LEARN TERRAFORM

Automate Multi-Cloud Infrastructure with Scalability

Diego Rodrigues

LEARN TERRAFORM
Automate Multi-Cloud Infrastructure with Scalability

2025 Edition

Author: Diego Rodrigues

studiod21portoalegre@gmail.com

Published by StudioD21.

Important Note

The codes and scripts presented in this book are primarily intended to illustrate, in a practical way, the concepts discussed throughout the chapters. They were developed to demonstrate didactic applications in controlled environments and may therefore require adaptations to work correctly in different contexts. It is the reader's responsibility to validate the specific configurations of their development environment before practical implementation.

More than providing ready-made solutions, this book seeks to encourage a solid understanding of the covered fundamentals, promoting critical thinking and technical autonomy. The presented examples should be seen as starting points for the reader to develop their own original solutions, adapted to the real demands of their career or projects. True technical competence arises from the ability to internalize essential principles and apply them creatively, strategically, and transformatively.

We therefore encourage each reader to go beyond mere reproduction of the examples, using this content as a foundation to build codes and scripts with their own identity, capable of generating significant impact in their professional journey. This is the spirit of applied knowledge: to learn deeply in order to innovate with purpose.

We thank you for your trust and wish you a productive and inspiring learning journey.

CONTENTS

GREETINGS

It is with great enthusiasm that I welcome you to a complete immersion into the world of Terraform, one of the most transformative tools in the infrastructure as code landscape. Your decision to explore this topic demonstrates not only technical curiosity but also a strategic mindset toward today's market demands—where automation, scalability, and governance have become essential requirements for any competitive digital operation.

In this book, LEARN TERRAFORM – Automate Multi-Cloud Infrastructure with Scalability, you will find a carefully crafted approach to guide you from basic understanding to practical and advanced application, covering the critical points that make a difference in real-world environments. The content has been developed to serve both professionals at the start of their journey and specialists seeking to expand their skills, bringing clarity and depth to every stage of the learning process.

Each chapter was built around three fundamental pillars: technical precision, practical applicability, and didactic progression. You will learn everything from the initial Terraform configuration, through the creation and management of resources across different cloud providers, integration with tools such as Kubernetes, Jenkins, Prometheus, Airflow, and Ansible, to more advanced topics like cost optimization, efficient modularization, multi-cloud strategies, and the application of security and compliance best practices.

What makes this book special is not just the content it delivers, but the way it is structured: with absolute attention to clarity, reading flow, and immediate impact on your day-to-day work. Each section is designed to be practical and applicable, offering not only concepts and commands but also real-world examples, detailed explanations, complex scenarios translated into accessible solutions, and sections dedicated to troubleshooting common errors, allowing you to move forward with confidence, safety, and technical mastery.

By dedicating yourself to this reading, you are placing yourself at the forefront of the movement that is reshaping the role of infrastructure within organizations. Mastering Terraform goes far beyond provisioning virtual machines, networks, and databases: it transforms how teams collaborate, how operations scale, and how companies respond to challenges and opportunities in the market. In a context where agility, resilience, and efficiency have become watchwords, the ability to automate and manage complex environments with Terraform translates into real competitive advantage.

This book was developed to be a reliable companion, whether you are an infrastructure engineer, a solutions architect, an operations analyst, a DevOps specialist, or a professional transitioning careers seeking to position yourself in an increasingly automation-driven landscape. It is not limited to being a technical manual—it serves as a strategic guide, helping you understand how decisions made in code impact operations, business, and above all, innovation.

Get ready to embark on a journey that will equip you not only with commands and scripts but with the understanding necessary to turn technology into concrete results. This book was built to broaden your vision, strengthen your technical skills, and provide valuable insights that can be applied to projects of any size and complexity.

Mastering Terraform means more than learning a tool: it means adopting a modern mindset focused on continuous delivery, quality, and innovation. It means taking an active role in building digital operations that not only work but make a positive impact, enabling organizations to be more agile, robust, and aligned with global best practices.

Thank you for choosing this book as your companion on this journey. I hope that by the end of this reading, you will have not only acquired technical knowledge but also inspiration to challenge standards, improve processes, and explore new possibilities. May this reading be not only useful but also motivating, and may it mark an important step in your professional journey.

Welcome, and have a transformative reading experience!

ABOUT THE AUTHOR

Diego Rodrigues
Technical Author and Independent Researcher
ORCID: https://orcid.org/0009-0006-2178-634X
StudioD21 Smart Tech Content & Intell Systems
E-mail: studiod21portoalegre@gmail.com
LinkedIn: www.linkedin.com/in/diegoxpertai

International technical author (tech writer) focused on the structured production of applied knowledge. He is the founder of StudioD21 Smart Tech Content & Intell Systems, where he leads the creation of intelligent frameworks and the publication of didactic technical books supported by artificial intelligence, such as the Kali Linux Extreme series, SMARTBOOKS D21, among others.

Holder of 42 international certifications issued by institutions such as IBM, Google, Microsoft, AWS, Cisco, META, Ec-Council, Palo Alto, and Boston University, he works in the fields of Artificial Intelligence, Machine Learning, Data Science, Big Data, Blockchain, Connectivity Technologies, Ethical Hacking, and Threat Intelligence.

Since 2003, he has developed over 200 technical projects for brands in Brazil, the USA, and Mexico. In 2024, he established himself as one of the most prominent technical authors of the new generation, with over 180 titles published in six languages. His work is based on his proprietary TECHWRITE 2.2 applied technical writing protocol, aimed at scalability, conceptual precision, and practical applicability in professional environments.

BOOK PRESENTATION

We live in a constantly evolving technological landscape, where infrastructure, operations, and development are increasingly integrated. In this dynamic environment, automation has moved beyond being just a trend to becoming an indispensable strategic element—and Terraform holds a central position in this movement. More than just a tool, Terraform represents a paradigm shift: it redefines the way we provision resources, structure environments, manage dependencies, and scale cloud operations.

This book was conceived to offer complete and progressive training, guiding the reader through all the necessary steps to master infrastructure as code with confidence and efficiency. It not only teaches commands and syntax but builds a strategic vision of how to apply Terraform in real-world contexts, aligning technical practices with business, security, cost, and scalability demands.

The content structure was designed with attention to the logical progression of learning, starting from solid foundations and gradually advancing to increasingly complex topics. The starting point introduces the essential concepts that shape Terraform's purpose and operation, helping the reader understand not just "what" to do but "why" to do it. In the opening chapters, the reader will find an introduction to the tool, learning about the ecosystem, the benefits of its adoption, the possibilities for integration, and the real impacts it generates on operations.

As the journey advances, the book dives into installation,

environment setup, initial commands, and the early best practices that ensure a robust foundation. This beginning lays the groundwork for exploring fundamental concepts— providers, resources, variables, outputs, modules, and state —that form the backbone of Terraform operations. Efficient modularization, addressed in specific chapters, emerges as a game changer for projects that grow in size and complexity, making maintenance predictable and scalability practical.

From there, the reader is guided into real-world integration scenarios. In-depth coverage will be given to provisioning practices in public clouds such as AWS, Google Cloud, and Azure, enabling the reader to understand how to apply the tool across multiple contexts and architectures. These chapters offer detailed examples of how to provision virtual machines, networks, databases, buckets, snapshots, and Kubernetes clusters—always with close attention to security, performance, and optimized resource usage.

The book then moves on to indispensable topics in the modern ecosystem: integration with tools such as Jenkins, Ansible, Airflow, Prometheus, Grafana, MLflow, and Helm, offering a broad view of how Terraform fits into CI/CD pipelines, MLOps, observability, and workflow automation. The reader will be introduced not only to the configuration of these integrations but also to their practical application in real day-to-day operations.

Following the commitment to deliver robust and applicable content, the book dedicates chapters to security and compliance, discussing policies, roles, validation, linting, sensitive data protection, and practices to meet corporate and regulatory standards. Next, advanced diagnostics and debugging practices are covered, focusing on logs, failure analysis, and external tools, preparing the reader to handle incidents and reduce operational response times.

Scalability and performance appear as central themes toward

the end of the book, discussing script tuning, parallel management, resource optimization, and strategies for complex environments. Cost optimization topics in the cloud are also covered, exploring cost analysis, smart use of tags and labels, and the application of practices that help align operations with financial efficiency.

The technical conclusion of the book presents case studies from real projects, including multi-cloud architectures and the DataExtreme project, exemplifying the practical application of the learned concepts, the pitfalls encountered, the solutions adopted, and the lessons drawn from these challenges.

The content of each chapter was developed according to the TECHWRITE 2.3 protocol, ensuring clarity, technical rigor, and immediate applicability. In all chapters, the reader will find:

- essential concepts,

- validated practical examples,

- common error resolution sections,

- recommended best practices,

- and a strategic summary that connects technique and purpose.

The book was designed to serve both individual study and team training, technical courses, corporate training programs, and quick reference in daily operations. All content was carefully prepared to ensure that its use adheres to ethical principles, reinforcing that infrastructure automation should be carried out with responsibility, respect for security, and alignment with global best practices.

Regardless of your current level of experience—whether you

are a curious beginner or an experienced professional seeking technical consolidation—this book was built to expand your capabilities. It is not just a repository of commands and examples: it was designed to help you develop a broad, operational, and strategic understanding, enabling you to integrate Terraform into your work environment in a mature and efficient manner.

Here, each section was crafted to deliver real value. The examples were not included merely as technical demonstrations but to teach the logic behind decisions, show the practical consequences of configurations, and anticipate problems that arise in everyday tool use. The goal is to enable you not just to repeat commands but to deeply understand Terraform's workings and become capable of adapting it to diverse contexts.

This book also serves as a guide for building technical culture within teams. It provides fundamentals that help create standards, establish governance, reduce errors, accelerate deliveries, and increase collaboration between development, operations, and security teams. It is, therefore, a work designed not only for individual learning but to generate collective impact, helping to raise the standard of operations as a whole.

Finally, the work invites the reader to look to the future. As Terraform evolves, new integrations, new practices, and new challenges emerge. This book does not aim to be an endpoint but rather a starting point, so that you, the reader, are prepared to innovate, question, improve processes, and above all, transform technology into a driver of results.

You are about to embark on a journey that combines technical depth, practical purpose, and strategic vision. May this reading not be just a passage through the world of Terraform, but a transformative experience that broadens your professional reach and strengthens your contribution to the challenges of today and tomorrow.

Welcome to the construction of modern, intelligent, and

resilient operations. Here, Terraform is the means—the impact you generate with it will be the true differentiator.

CHAPTER 1. INTRODUCTION TO TERRAFORM

Terraform is a robust infrastructure as code (IaC) tool, designed to enable the provisioning, management, and versioning of infrastructure in an efficient, secure, and reproducible manner. From cloud environments to on-premises services, Terraform offers a declarative approach to describing the desired configuration, eliminating the need for repetitive manual tasks. The essence of Terraform lies in transforming infrastructure into code that can be versioned, reviewed, shared, and automated, promoting consistency and reducing operational errors.

Infrastructure as Code (IaC) has revolutionized the way technology teams manage their environments, allowing infrastructure to be treated with the same discipline as application source code. This approach ensures that any infrastructure modification is traceable, reviewable, and, above all, replicable. Instead of manually creating virtual machines, networks, or databases, professionals define these structures in configuration files that Terraform interprets to perform automatic provisioning. This drastically reduces time spent on repetitive operations and minimizes the risk of human error.

The benefits of Terraform go far beyond basic automation. It enables:

- Consistency in provisioning across multiple environments, ensuring that development, staging, and production are identical.

- Full versioning of infrastructure configurations, allowing easy rollback to previous states.

- Collaboration among teams, since configuration files can be shared and reviewed like any other code artifact.

- Operational scalability, enabling the management of everything from small applications to complex, enterprise-level, multi-cloud architectures.

- Integration with CI/CD tools for continuous delivery pipeline automation.

The Terraform ecosystem is broad and well-established. It connects to a vast array of providers such as AWS, Azure, Google Cloud, Kubernetes, VMware, among others, through modules called providers. Each provider implements the necessary interface to interact with the specific APIs of supported platforms. This means that with a single set of tools and practices, you can manage virtually any type of digital resource required for modern organizational operations.

Another fundamental pillar of Terraform is its declarative model. Unlike tools that use imperative approaches, in Terraform you describe the desired state of the infrastructure, and the internal engine automatically determines the actions needed to achieve it. This simplifies operations such as adding, updating, or removing resources, as the user does not need to specify in detail how the changes will be applied.

The basic Terraform execution process follows the cycle: init, plan, apply, and destroy. The init step initializes the project by downloading the necessary plugins and modules. The plan command generates an execution plan showing which changes will be applied, providing predictability and control.

The apply command executes the generated plan, applying the modifications to the infrastructure. Finally, the destroy command removes all created resources, useful for avoiding unnecessary costs or maintaining clean environments.

Terraform's use cases are extensive. It is used to provision Kubernetes clusters, EC2 servers on AWS, virtual machines on Azure, data pipelines on Google Cloud, virtual private clouds (VPCs), managed databases, storage systems, serverless applications, machine learning environments, among others. Additionally, organizations use Terraform to implement advanced governance, cost control, compliance, and security practices.

Resource configuration is done through files with the .tf extension, written in HashiCorp Configuration Language (HCL), a simple, readable, and powerful language. A .tf file can describe, for example, the provisioning of a virtual machine with its characteristics, association to a specific network, firewall rules, and outputs that will be used in other parts of the project. This flexibility allows configurations to be encapsulated into modules, promoting reuse and modularization of definitions— fundamental in medium and large-scale projects.

Terraform maintains a state file, which stores the current state of the infrastructure. This file allows the tool to know exactly which resources already exist, which need to be updated, and which should be removed. This mechanism is essential to avoid inconsistencies and ensure the environment accurately reflects the code definitions. When working in teams, it is recommended to use remote backends to store the state, ensuring locking and avoiding conflicts during concurrent executions.

In the context of modern organizations, adopting Terraform generates significant impacts. Operations teams can drastically reduce provisioning time, developers gain autonomy to create temporary environments for testing, and the security team gains greater visibility and control over the infrastructure. Additionally, integration with tools like GitHub Actions, GitLab CI, Jenkins, Ansible, and Prometheus enables the construction of sophisticated automation, monitoring, and governance pipelines.

A relevant point in the Terraform ecosystem is Terraform Cloud, a SaaS offering that provides centralized state management, remote execution, team collaboration, compliance policies, and integration with GitOps workflows. Terraform Cloud eliminates backend infrastructure concerns and allows IaC practices to scale at the organizational level.

Adopting best practices from the start is crucial. It is recommended to:

- Modularize configurations to avoid duplication and facilitate reuse.

- Use variables to make scripts flexible and reusable.

- Protect the state file, especially when it contains sensitive information.

- Implement code review for configuration changes.

- Automate the full cycle through CI/CD pipelines.

Despite the initial learning curve, Terraform consistently delivers gains over time. It reduces the dependence on complex imperative scripts, minimizes the chance of human error, and enables environment standardization, accelerating organizations' DevOps journey.

Among the main challenges faced by new users are understanding the declarative model, efficiently organizing the state, and creating well-structured modules. These aspects will be explored in depth in the upcoming chapters, ensuring progressive evolution in mastering best practices.

Additionally, Terraform promotes important cultural alignment within organizations. It encourages declarative thinking, transparency in changes, and collaboration among diverse professional profiles such as developers, data engineers, security analysts, and cloud architects. This synergy strengthens the DevOps culture and lays the groundwork for more advanced initiatives, such as intelligent automation, dynamic autoscaling, advanced observability, and FinOps practices.

Terraform also stands out for its ability to integrate with complementary tools. For example, combining it with Ansible allows for detailed configuration of provisioned machines, while integration with Helm facilitates Kubernetes application deployments. Joint use with Prometheus and Grafana enables monitoring and visualization of critical metrics from provisioned infrastructure, creating a robust and cohesive ecosystem.

Another distinguishing feature of Terraform is its active and vibrant community. There is a vast array of prebuilt modules available in the Terraform Registry, accelerating projects and incorporating best practices consolidated by the global community. The community also contributes tutorials, examples, forum discussions, and continuous improvements to the tool's core.

Terraform's use is not limited to large companies or complex projects. Small teams, startups, and individual developers find in it a powerful solution to quickly and consistently create environments, eliminating friction in the development cycle. Whether creating a local Kubernetes cluster for testing, provisioning a serverless application on AWS, or setting up complex pipelines in hybrid environments, Terraform flexibly adapts to a wide range of needs.

In an era of accelerated digital transformation, where agility is a competitive factor, Terraform emerges as a strategic asset.

It enables rapid experimentation, on-demand scalability, and operational cost reduction while strengthening the pillars of security and governance.

Strategic Summary

- Terraform is a declarative Infrastructure as Code tool that transforms how organizations provision, manage, and version infrastructure.

- It offers benefits such as consistency across environments, configuration versioning, enhanced collaboration, operational scalability, and CI/CD integration.

- Its ecosystem includes multiple providers, reusable modules, state mechanisms, and advanced integrations with tools like Ansible, Helm, Prometheus, Grafana, Jenkins, and Terraform Cloud.

- The declarative model allows describing the desired state of infrastructure, with Terraform calculating and applying the necessary changes.

- Both small and large organizations find in Terraform an adaptable, powerful, and indispensable solution to accelerate the DevOps journey, promote operational efficiency, and ensure governance.

- The global Terraform community provides ready-to-use modules, best practices, and ongoing support, enabling beginner and advanced users to evolve rapidly in using the tool.

From this point, we will move on to installing Terraform, initial configuration, and running the first command, preparing the ground for the next steps toward automation and orchestration of infrastructure with technical excellence.

CHAPTER 2. INSTALLING TERRAFORM

The first step to mastering Terraform is to ensure that it is correctly installed and configured in your work environment. Although installing Terraform is a relatively simple process, it involves some crucial details that ensure the tool runs smoothly and avoids future headaches. We will explore everything from download and installation to running the first command, also covering the most common beginner errors, recommended best practices, and a strategic summary that ties all the points together.

Download and Installation

Terraform is distributed as a single binary, which greatly simplifies its installation since it does not rely on complex packages or additional libraries. To download it, visit the official Terraform website at https://www.terraform.io/downloads.html. There you will find versions for different operating systems, including Windows, macOS, Linux, and FreeBSD, as well as for 32-bit and 64-bit architectures. It is always recommended to download the latest version, as it contains security fixes, new features, and performance improvements.

After downloading the file corresponding to your operating system, unzip the ZIP or TAR.GZ package into a folder of your choice. The content will be a single executable called terraform. By default, it does not come with a graphical installer or installation scripts, meaning the next step is to manually configure the system PATH so the terminal recognizes the terraform command from any directory.

On Windows, after unzipping the binary, move it to an appropriate folder, such as C:\Terraform, or keep it in the extracted folder. Then, open Control Panel → System → Advanced Settings → Environment Variables. Edit the Path variable and add the full path where the executable was placed. Click OK to confirm.

On macOS and Linux, unzip the binary into a folder like /usr/local/bin or another folder already included in the PATH. If you prefer to use a custom folder, for example ~/terraform, you will need to manually add this folder to the PATH by editing the shell configuration file, such as .bashrc, .bash_profile, .zshrc, or .profile, depending on the shell used. An example of the command to add to the PATH is:

ruby

```
export PATH=$PATH:/path/to/terraform
```

After editing and saving the file, run source ~/.bashrc (or the equivalent for your shell) to reload the settings.

PATH Configuration

Correctly configuring the PATH ensures that the terminal recognizes the terraform command in any directory. A quick test to check if the PATH is properly set is to open a new terminal and type:

nginx

```
terraform -v
```

The terminal should display the installed Terraform version.

If you receive an error message saying the command was not found, this indicates that the PATH was not correctly configured. In such cases, go back to the previous step, review the specified path, and make sure it points directly to the folder containing the executable.

It is worth noting that PATH changes made via the terminal only take effect in the current session. To make them permanent, it is essential to include them in the shell configuration files, ensuring they persist after restarts.

First Command

With Terraform installed and the PATH correctly configured, it's time to run the first command to ensure the tool is working as expected. Create a test folder on your system, for example terraform-test, and inside it, create a file called main.tf with the following basic content:

nginx

```
terraform {
  required_version = ">= 1.0.0"
}
```

This file defines the minimum required Terraform version. In the terminal, navigate to the folder where the file was created and run:

csharp

```
terraform init
```

The init command initializes the working directory, downloads the necessary providers, and prepares the environment for execution. You should see messages indicating successful initialization, including plugin downloads.

Next, run:

nginx

```
terraform plan
```

This command generates an execution plan, showing what actions would be performed (even if, in this example, no concrete changes will occur). Finally, run:

nginx

```
terraform apply
```

This command applies the changes described in the configuration file. In the current example, since no resources are defined, Terraform will simply confirm that nothing was altered.

Congratulations: you have completed the installation, configuration, and execution of Terraform's first basic cycle.

Common Error Resolution

Error: The 'terraform' command is not recognized in the terminal.
Solution: Check if the PATH is correctly configured. Make sure the specified path points directly to the folder where the Terraform executable is located and that the PATH changes were applied correctly.

Error: Permission denied when running the binary on Linux or macOS.
Solution: Ensure the file has execution permissions. Use the command `chmod +x terraform` in the directory where the binary is located to make it executable.

Error: Version conflict between Terraform and providers.
Solution: Check the required_version block in the main.tf file and ensure it matches the installed Terraform version. If necessary, update the configuration or download a compatible version.

Error: Failed to initialize the backend during terraform init.
Solution: Review the backend configurations specified in the configuration file. Ensure the access credentials (for example, AWS, Azure, GCP) are correct and that the remote resources exist.

Error: Internet connection failure during provider download.
Solution: Confirm that the machine is connected to the internet and that there are no firewall or proxy blocks preventing the download. If behind a proxy, configure the HTTP_PROXY and HTTPS_PROXY environment variables.

Error: Invalid configuration file or syntax error in .tf.
Solution: Use the command terraform validate to check the integrity and syntax of the configuration file. Carefully review error messages, as they usually indicate the exact location of the problem.

Best Practices

- Always use the latest Terraform version unless you need specific compatibility.

- Keep configurations versioned in a version control system like Git.

- Modularize your configurations from the start, separating resources into reusable modules.

- Use variables to make definitions more flexible and adaptable to different environments.

- Protect the terraform.tfstate file using remote backends with locking enabled, avoiding state corruption in collaborative environments.

- Automate the complete cycle with CI/CD pipelines to prevent untraceable manual executions.

- Document your configurations with clear and consistent comments, making future maintenance easier.

- Perform code reviews (pull requests) for significant infrastructure definition changes.

- Test your configurations in staging environments before applying them to production.

- Adopt consistent naming conventions to facilitate resource identification and organization.

Strategic Summary

Correctly installing Terraform is the first step to unlocking its full potential in infrastructure automation and management. The process starts with downloading the binary from the official site, followed by unzipping and configuring the PATH, ensuring the terminal recognizes the terraform command. Once this step is complete, the first command cycle (init, plan, apply) serves as a practical check that the tool is operating correctly.

The most common installation errors are usually related to PATH configurations, permissions, version conflicts, and internet connectivity issues. Knowing these failures and their solutions can save hours of frustration and speed up tool adoption. Additionally, adopting best practices such as modularization, versioning, variable use, CI/CD automation, and code review ensures that Terraform projects grow sustainably and securely.

Correctly installing Terraform is not just a technical step but also a cultural milestone. It signals the adoption of modern infrastructure as code practices, strengthening team collaboration, increasing change predictability, and promoting operational excellence. By mastering this foundation, you will be ready to move on to more complex challenges, such as multi-cloud management, DevOps pipeline integration, and the implementation of advanced governance and security strategies.

With Terraform ready to use, the next step will be to explore its capabilities in depth, creating real resources and building resilient architectures that support the demands of modern organizations. Each learned command, each resolved error, and each applied best practice will contribute to turning your Terraform journey into a story of efficiency, continuous learning, and significant organizational impact.

CHAPTER 3. FUNDAMENTAL CONCEPTS

Terraform is much more than just an automation tool: it is a complete ecosystem for defining, provisioning, and managing infrastructure declaratively. To use it effectively, it's essential to understand its fundamental concepts. In this chapter, we will explore the core elements that form the foundation of Terraform — providers, resources, variables, outputs, modules, and state — and how all these building blocks fit into the basic execution cycle. We will also cover the most common errors that arise at this stage and the best practices that ensure the longevity and scalability of Terraform projects. Finally, we'll present a strategic summary that connects these learnings to the goal of building reliable and replicable environments.

Providers, Resources, Variables, Outputs

Providers are the components that allow Terraform to interact with external services. A provider is responsible for managing communication with the API of a particular service, such as AWS, Azure, Google Cloud, Kubernetes, VMware, GitHub, Cloudflare, among many others. By adding a provider to the configuration file, Terraform automatically downloads the corresponding plugin during initialization with terraform init. For example, to use AWS, simply declare in the .tf file:

nginx

```
provider "aws" {
  region = "us-east-1"
```

```
}
```

This configuration informs Terraform that the resources defined in the project will use the AWS provider, specifically in the us-east-1 region.

Resources are the blocks that describe the actual elements we want to create and manage — virtual machines, networks, databases, storage buckets, firewall rules, among others. A resource follows the pattern:

nginx

```
resource "aws_instance" "example" {
  ami         = "ami-0c55b159cbfafe1f0"
  instance_type = "t2.micro"
}
```

In this example, we are creating an EC2 virtual machine in AWS with a specified image and instance type. The logical name example is used to reference the resource in other parts of the code.

Variables provide a way to parameterize configurations, making them flexible and reusable. Variables help avoid repeating hardcoded values in the code and make it easier to adapt to multiple environments. Variables can be defined in separate files (variables.tf) or in the same configuration file, using:

go

```
variable "instance_type" {
  type    = string
  default = "t2.micro"
```

}

In the resource, we can reference the variable with var.instance_type. This makes it easy to modify the value in different contexts, using .tfvars files or command-line parameters.

Outputs are used to expose useful information generated by Terraform after provisioning. These outputs can include, for example, the IP address of a created machine, the endpoint of a load balancer, or the URL of a bucket. They help with integration with other tools and communication between modules:

nginx

```
output "instance_ip" {
  value = aws_instance.example.public_ip
}
```

When running terraform apply, Terraform will display the output value in the terminal, making it easy to quickly access critical information.

Modules and State

Modules are reusable collections of Terraform configurations grouped in directories. They allow related resources to be encapsulated, promoting organization, modularity, and reuse. A module can be local (within the same repository), remote (stored in a Git repository, bucket, or registry), or official (available in the Terraform Registry).

For example, we can create a module called vpc that contains all the logic to create a VPC, subnets, gateways, and routing tables. In our main file, we reference the module like this:

nginx

```
module "vpc" {
  source = "./modules/vpc"
  cidr_block = "10.0.0.0/16"
}
```

This makes projects more organized and easier to maintain, as changes in the modules affect all instances where they are used.

State is the file that stores the current state of the infrastructure managed by Terraform. It contains a detailed mapping between the resources defined in the .tf files and the actual resources in the cloud provider. This file, called terraform.tfstate, allows Terraform to know exactly what needs to be created, updated, or destroyed.

Proper state management is critical, especially in teams. It's recommended to use remote backends such as Terraform Cloud, S3 with DynamoDB (AWS), or Google Cloud Storage to store state securely, prevent corruption, and enable operation locking during simultaneous runs.

Basic Execution Cycle

The basic Terraform cycle involves four main commands:

- terraform init → Initializes the project, downloads providers, and prepares the environment.

- terraform plan → Generates an execution plan showing the actions to be taken.

- terraform apply → Applies the changes to the environment as per the generated plan.

- terraform destroy → Dismantles the provisioned infrastructure, useful for cleaning up environments.

This cycle ensures predictability and control over changes. plan helps validate what will be altered before applying, while destroy allows the removal of resources no longer needed.

Example of a complete cycle:

csharp

```
terraform init

terraform plan -out=tfplan

terraform apply tfplan

terraform destroy
```

Common Error Resolution

Error: Provider not found or download failed.
Solution: Run terraform init again to force plugin download. Check your internet connection and the configuration file.

Error: Invalid syntax in .tf files.
Solution: Use terraform validate to identify and correct syntax issues. Also check braces, brackets, and indentation.

Error: Undefined variable value.
Solution: Ensure all required variables are defined, either in the code, in a .tfvars file, or as a command-line parameter with -var.

Error: Corrupted or inconsistent state.
Solution: Back up the terraform.tfstate file. If necessary, use terraform state to directly manipulate the state, removing invalid entries.

Error: State lock in remote backend.
Solution: Check if another user or pipeline is running an operation. If the lock persists, use the unlock commands provided by the backend, such as terraform force-unlock.

Error: Duplicate resources or name conflicts.
Solution: Carefully review logical names and resource keys. Maintain a clear naming convention to avoid collisions.

Error: Unresolved dependencies between resources.
Solution: Explicitly use the depends_on argument to declare dependencies between resources that are not automatically inferred.

Best Practices

- Modularize infrastructure into small reusable components, reducing coupling and increasing maintainability.

- Use clear and consistent names for resources, modules, variables, and outputs.

- Keep all files versioned in Git, ensuring traceability and change history.

- Separate environments (development, staging, production) into distinct workspaces or directories.

- Use .tfvars files to store environment-specific values.

- Document modules and resources to facilitate team collaboration.

- Configure remote backends to store state securely.

- Adopt CI/CD pipelines to validate and apply changes automatically.

- Always run terraform plan before terraform apply to review changes.

- Use the lifecycle feature to control the recreation or protection of critical resources.

Strategic Summary

The fundamental concepts of Terraform form the backbone of any infrastructure-as-code project. Understanding providers, resources, variables, outputs, modules, and state is essential to fully harness the tool's capabilities. Providers connect Terraform to the external world, resources define what will be managed, variables and outputs provide flexibility and visibility, modules enable organization and reuse, and state ensures everything stays aligned between code and reality.

Mastering the basic execution cycle — init, plan, apply, destroy — gives users the necessary control to operate confidently in any environment. The most common errors can be quickly resolved with the right approaches, avoiding wasted time and preventing critical failures. Best practices ensure that the code remains clean, organized, and ready to scale.

Beyond the technical layer, these concepts have a profound cultural impact. They foster collaboration between developers, operations engineers, and architects, promote transparency in changes, and encourage a mindset of automation and continuous improvement. Organizations that adopt these practices gain agility, security, governance, and innovation capability.

With these foundations in hand, you'll be ready to advance to more sophisticated topics, such as multi-cloud environment management, integration with external tools, advanced modularization strategies, and change control at an organizational scale. Each concept learned here will be a key piece in building resilient, efficient, and market-aligned infrastructures.

CHAPTER 4. FIRST TERRAFORM SCRIPT

The first hands-on experience with Terraform usually happens when we create our own .tf script. This moment marks the transition from conceptual learning to real execution, where we understand how to transform code into functional infrastructure. Writing, validating, and applying a script correctly not only consolidates the theory learned but also reveals important nuances about the tool. This module explores the basic structure of a .tf file, the full init/plan/apply/destroy execution cycle, the script validation process, common errors faced, and recommended best practices. At the end, a strategic summary will connect all the points to ensure you move forward confidently to the next challenges.

.tf Structure

Terraform uses files with the .tf extension to define infrastructure as code. These files are written in HashiCorp Configuration Language (HCL), a declarative, easy-to-read, modular, and flexible language. The basic structure of a .tf file generally includes the following blocks:

- provider → Specifies the infrastructure provider to be used, such as AWS, Azure, Google Cloud, or others.

- resource → Defines the resources to be created, modified, or destroyed. This can be a virtual machine, database, network, load balancer, etc.

- variable → Declares reusable variables to parameterize the code, making it dynamic and adaptable to different environments.

- output → Exposes relevant information after provisioning, such as IPs, resource names, URLs.

- module → Groups reusable code blocks, allowing organization and standardization of configurations.

A basic example of a .tf file would be:

nginx

```
provider "aws" {
  region = "us-east-1"
}


resource "aws_instance" "web" {
  ami        = "ami-0c55b159cbfafe1f0"
  instance_type = "t2.micro"
}


output "instance_ip" {
  value = aws_instance.web.public_ip
}
```

This script instructs Terraform to use the AWS provider, create an EC2 virtual machine with a defined image and instance type, and display the public IP address as an output.

init/plan/apply/destroy

With the script ready, the classic Terraform execution cycle begins:

- terraform init
  Initializes the working directory. This command downloads the necessary plugins, configures the backend, and prepares the environment for operation. It should always be run when a new project is created or when there are changes to providers and modules.

- terraform plan
  Generates an execution plan showing all actions to be taken to align the current state with the desired state. This command does not modify anything in the real infrastructure; it only shows what will be done.

- terraform apply
  Applies the changes described in the plan. This command provisions, updates, or destroys cloud resources as specified in the script. Before executing, Terraform requests confirmation, ensuring that no unexpected changes occur.

- terraform destroy
  Destroys all resources managed by Terraform in that directory. This command is useful for cleaning up temporary environments and avoiding unnecessary costs.

A complete cycle in practice:

csharp

```
terraform init
terraform plan -out=tfplan
```

```
terraform apply tfplan
terraform destroy
```

This flow reinforces the discipline of anticipating changes before applying them, reducing the risk of errors.

Script Validation

Validating the script before performing destructive operations is a critical step. Terraform offers the command:

nginx

```
terraform validate
```

This command checks whether the syntax of the .tf files is correct and whether the blocks are organized as expected. It does not assess the script's logic or interact with providers but is effective in detecting structural errors.

In addition to validate, using:

bash

```
terraform fmt
```

standardizes code formatting, ensuring readability and consistency across files. This practice is especially important in teams, as it reduces divergences during code reviews.

To validate logic and check dependencies, use terraform plan. It allows simulating the execution and identifying gaps before making changes to the real environment.

Common Error Resolution

Error: terraform init command failed due to provider issues.
Solution: Check the provider block configuration. Confirm that the version is available and that there is network connectivity. Run terraform init again after correcting the problem.

Error: Syntax failure in .tf file.
Solution: Run terraform validate and correct the indicated sections. Pay attention to braces, brackets, quotes, and indentation.

Error: Required variable values not defined.
Solution: Define required variables using .tfvars files or by passing values via the command line with -var. Check that the variables were correctly declared.

Error: Implicit dependencies not recognized.
Solution: Use depends_on in the affected resource to ensure the correct execution order.

Error: Execution fails due to insufficient permissions.
Solution: Review the credentials used in the provider. Ensure the credentials have permissions to create, modify, and delete the desired resources.

Error: Plan and state inconsistent.
Solution: Regenerate the plan with terraform plan and, if necessary, re-run terraform apply. In critical cases, use terraform refresh to synchronize the state.

Error: Problems with shared state in a team.
Solution: Configure a remote backend with locking enabled. This avoids simultaneous changes that could corrupt the state.

Best Practices

- Keep .tf files organized by functionality, e.g., network.tf, compute.tf, outputs.tf.

- Use variables to parameterize sensitive and dynamic

values.

- Include outputs only when they are truly necessary for integration with other systems.

- Regularly use the terraform fmt command to maintain code consistency.

- Implement modules to reuse configurations across different projects.

- Store the terraform.tfstate file in remote backends with locking enabled, especially in collaborative environments.

- Use workspaces to separate environments such as development, staging, and production.

- Adopt tags and labels on resources to facilitate tracking, organization, and governance.

- Conduct code reviews in pull requests to identify issues before applying changes.

- Never run terraform apply directly in production without carefully reviewing the execution plan.

Strategic Summary

Writing and applying the first Terraform script is an essential milestone in learning the tool. It transforms concepts into practice, consolidating understanding of providers, resources, variables, and outputs. Properly structuring the .tf file, combined with the disciplined init/plan/apply/destroy cycle, establishes a solid foundation for any infrastructure-as-code project.

Script validation, both at the syntax level (validate) and logic level (plan), drastically reduces the occurrence of errors and builds confidence in operations. By addressing common errors with precise solutions, the user develops resilience and sharpens their troubleshooting skills — a fundamental ability in the DevOps world.

Best practices elevate the maturity of Terraform projects, making them more readable, secure, scalable, and aligned with corporate demands. With the adoption of clear standards, modularization, and versioning, teams can evolve quickly while maintaining quality and predictability.

Beyond the technical dimension, the first Terraform script opens the door to an important cultural shift: it immerses the professional in an ecosystem where infrastructure is treated as code, reinforcing principles of automation, traceability, and continuous improvement. This alignment not only increases operational efficiency but also paves the way for advanced initiatives such as GitOps, FinOps, security as code, and platform engineering.

CHAPTER 5. VARIABLES AND OUTPUTS

The use of variables and outputs in Terraform is a turning point between simple scripts and truly scalable, reusable solutions. When applied well, these two elements make code dynamic, adaptable to different environments, and much easier to maintain. At this moment we will dives deep into the available variable types, the construction of reusable outputs, the use of external files to separate configurations, and the common errors associated with these practices. We will also present best practices to ensure consistency and security, and finally, a strategic summary that connects all this knowledge to the reality of professional projects.

Types of Variables

Variables in Terraform allow you to parameterize values, eliminating hardcoding and making scripts more flexible. They are declared in the variable block, usually in a separate file like variables.tf, although they can also be placed directly in the main .tf file. Variables can receive values from .tfvars files, from the command line, or from environment variables.

The main types of variables in Terraform are:

String

This is the simplest type, representing text values. Example:

```go
variable "region" {
```

```
  type   = string
  default = "us-east-1"
}
```

Number

Represents numeric values, such as the number of instances or disk sizes.
Example:

typescript

```
variable "instance_count" {
  type   = number
  default = 2
}
```

Bool

Stores boolean values, true or false, useful for enabling or disabling conditional resources.
Example:

go

```
variable "enable_monitoring" {
  type   = bool
  default = true
}
```

List

Stores an ordered sequence of values, usually of the same type.

Example:

go

```
variable "availability_zones" {
  type   = list(string)
  default = ["us-east-1a", "us-east-1b"]
}
```

Map

Stores key-value pairs, allowing configuration of multiple related attributes.
Example:

go

```
variable "tags" {
  type = map(string)
  default = {
    environment = "dev"
    owner     = "team"
  }
}
```

Object

Stores more complex structures composed of multiple attributes with different types.
Example:

typescript

```
variable "instance_config" {
```

```
  type = object({
    instance_type = string
    disk_size    = number
  })
  default = {
    instance_type = "t2.micro"
    disk_size    = 30
  }
}
```

Any

Accepts any type of value. Its use should be moderate, as it reduces static validation.
Example:

python

```
variable "dynamic_value" {
  type = any
}
```

Variable declaration in the main code:

java

```
resource "aws_instance" "web" {
  ami        = var.ami_id
  instance_type = var.instance_type
}
```

Reusable Outputs

Outputs are essential for exposing useful information from Terraform, whether to users, other modules, or external tools. They help make scripts more interoperable and improve integration between different infrastructure layers.

An output is declared like this:

nginx

```
output "instance_ip" {
  value = aws_instance.web.public_ip
}
```

Outputs can be consumed in external scripts or displayed directly in the terminal after terraform apply. When used in modules, they can be referenced by the main code:

lua

```
module "webserver" {
  source = "./modules/webserver"
}
```

```
output "webserver_ip" {
  value = module.webserver.instance_ip
}
```

Outputs are also useful in CI/CD pipelines, where the result of a Terraform execution can be used by subsequent steps, such as configuring a DNS, updating monitoring, or triggering application deployments.

Best practices for outputs:

- Expose only what is necessary, avoiding leaking sensitive data.

- Use clear and descriptive names.

- Document the purpose of each output in the code.

- Use sensitive = true for outputs that contain confidential information.

Variables in External Files

Managing variables directly in the main code can quickly become chaotic. To solve this, Terraform allows the use of .tfvars files to store values separated by environment, making the process organized and easy to maintain.

Example of variables.tf:

go

```
variable "region" {
  type = string
}
```

Example of dev.tfvars:

ini

```
region = "us-east-1"
```

Execution with the external variable file:

csharp

```
terraform apply -var-file=dev.tfvars
```

This approach offers several benefits:

- Facilitates switching between environments (dev, staging, prod).

- Centralizes dynamic configurations.

- Reduces risks of manual changes in code files.

- Allows versioning of values separate from the main code.

In addition to .tfvars, variables can be passed directly from the command line:

csharp

```
terraform apply -var="region=us-east-1"
```

Or via environment variables:

arduino

```
export TF_VAR_region=us-east-1
```

Common Error Resolution

Error: Required variable value not defined.
Solution: Make sure to define all required variables in the code, .tfvars, or as a command-line parameter.

Error: Incompatible type assigned to variable.
Solution: Check if the provided value matches the expected type (string, number, bool, list, map). Correct it in the .tfvars file or the command line.

Error: Output referencing non-existent resource.
Solution: Confirm that the referenced resource in the output exists and is correctly named. Run terraform validate to help detect this.

Error: Variable defined in multiple places with conflicting values.
Solution: Prioritize the order of definition — command line overrides .tfvars, which overrides default values in the code. Choose a single place to define critical variables.

Error: Failure to interpolate outputs between modules.
Solution: Ensure that outputs are correctly exposed in the modules and referenced in the main code using module.<name>.<output>.

Error: Exposure of sensitive data in outputs.
Solution: Use sensitive = true in outputs to mask their display in the terminal.

Best Practices

- Always define variables in separate files (variables.tf) to keep the code organized.

- Use .tfvars to store environment-specific values.

- Prefer descriptive names for variables and outputs, avoiding obscure abbreviations.

- Add description fields in variable declarations to facilitate maintenance.

- Avoid hardcoding sensitive values in the code; use environment variables or solutions like HashiCorp Vault.

- Use sensitive = true in outputs that expose passwords,

tokens, or private keys.

- Use lists and maps to group related values, reducing repetition.

- Organize .tfvars files by environment and keep them versioned in the repository (with care for sensitive values).

- Validate scripts with terraform validate before applying changes.

- Document the function of each variable and output in the project README or directly in the code.

Strategic Summary

Variables and outputs are fundamental pillars for transforming simple Terraform scripts into professional, scalable solutions. Variables allow you to create dynamic, flexible, and adaptable code across different contexts, while outputs expose essential data for integration, monitoring, and automation. Together, these two elements form the foundation for implementing advanced practices such as modularization, code reuse, CI/CD pipeline integration, and multi-environment management.

The variable types — string, number, bool, list, map, object, any — offer a powerful range of possibilities, enabling you to handle everything from basic configurations to complex structures. Well-planned outputs become strategic tools for connecting components, sharing data between modules, and feeding external processes.

The use of external .tfvars files further elevates project maturity, providing a clean separation between code and configuration and allowing for quick environment switching. This approach reduces risks, increases predictability, and makes infrastructure management more efficient.

Common errors related to variables and outputs generally stem from misconfiguration, incorrect typing, or definition conflicts. Knowing these pitfalls and their solutions helps avoid rework and accelerates the development flow.

Best practices — such as file separation, clear names, responsible handling of sensitive values, validation, and documentation — ensure that projects are sustainable, secure, and easy to evolve over time.

On a strategic level, mastering variables and outputs positions professionals for more advanced challenges, such as using public and private modules, integrating with secret management tools, dynamically configuring multiple environments, and collaborating efficiently in teams. This technical mastery, combined with a strategic vision, becomes a valuable competitive edge in projects of any size.

CHAPTER 6. MODULES IN TERRAFORM

The use of modules in Terraform represents a decisive leap in technical maturity and project organization for infrastructure as code. A module is essentially a container of reusable Terraform resources, designed to be referenced in multiple places with different parameters, maintaining consistency, scalability, and reducing duplication. By adopting modules, it's possible to transform complex configurations into reusable and isolated components, promoting standardization across environments and teams. We will explore here creating modules, applying them in different projects, presents a practical example with real execution, lists the most common errors related to modular structure, and concludes with best practices and a strategic summary.

Creating Modules

A module in Terraform is a collection of .tf files grouped in a directory, defining a set of resources and allowing parameterization through variables. Creating a module starts with identifying a functionality that will be used in multiple points of the project — for example, creating a VPC, a security group, or a set of EC2 instances.

To structure a module, we generally create three main files inside a directory:

- main.tf – where the resources are declared.

- variables.tf – where expected variables are defined.

- outputs.tf – where the values to be exposed by the module are specified.

For example, a module to create an EC2 instance might have the following content:

main.tf:

java

```
resource "aws_instance" "this" {
  ami       = var.ami
  instance_type = var.instance_type
  tags = {
    Name = var.instance_name
  }
}
```

variables.tf:

go

```
variable "ami" {
  description = "AMI ID to use for the instance"
  type    = string
}

variable "instance_type" {
  description = "Type of instance"
  type    = string
```

```
  default   = "t2.micro"
}


variable "instance_name" {
  description = "Name tag for the instance"
  type     = string
}
```

outputs.tf:

kotlin

```
output "public_ip" {
  value = aws_instance.this.public_ip
}
```

Once created, this module can be used in any main project as a module block:

nginx

```
module "webserver" {
  source     = "./modules/ec2_instance"
  ami       = "ami-0c55b159cbfafe1f0"
  instance_type = "t2.small"
  instance_name = "web-1"
}
```

The source directive can point to a local path, a Git repository, a remote bucket, or a public module from the Terraform Registry. This flexibility allows modules to be shared, versioned, and widely distributed across projects and teams.

Reuse Across Projects

The main advantage of modules is reuse. By encapsulating logical blocks of infrastructure, you can apply consistent patterns across different projects and environments. This eliminates the need to copy and paste configurations, facilitates maintenance, and avoids technical drift.

Reuse can be done in two ways:

Local Modules

These are stored in the same repository or folder structure of the current project. They are useful during development or when the module will not be shared externally.

nginx

```
module "sg_web" {
  source = "./modules/security_group_web"
  vpc_id = "vpc-123456"
}
```

Remote Modules

These are stored in Git repositories, S3 buckets, or the Terraform Registry. They allow explicit version control and are ideal for distributed teams.

nginx

```
module "vpc_shared" {
```

```
  source = "git::https://github.com/company/terraform-
modules.git//vpc"

  version = "v1.2.0"

}
```

Using versioning in remote modules is essential. It prevents real-time changes from impacting multiple projects simultaneously. With each module change, a new version is published, and each project decides when to adopt it.

Benefits of Reuse Across Projects

- Reduced rework.

- Standardization of configurations.

- Application of centralized best practices.

- Easier auditing and governance.

- Greater agility for new teams and environments.

Practical Example

Let's build a complete example using a local module to provision an EC2 instance with tags and public IP output.

1. Folder Structure

css

project/

```
├── main.tf
├── variables.tf
├── outputs.tf
└── modules/
    └── ec2_instance/
        ├── main.tf
        ├── variables.tf
        └── outputs.tf
```

2. **Module Content** (modules/ec2_instance/)
   main.tf:

java

```java
resource "aws_instance" "this" {
  ami           = var.ami
  instance_type = var.instance_type

  tags = {
    Name        = var.name
    Environment = var.environment
  }
}
```

variables.tf:

go

```
variable "ami" {
  type = string
}


variable "instance_type" {
  type   = string
  default = "t2.micro"
}


variable "name" {
  type = string
}


variable "environment" {
  type = string
}
```

outputs.tf:

kotlin

```
output "instance_ip" {
  value = aws_instance.this.public_ip
}
```

3. Main Project Code
main.tf:

nginx

```
provider "aws" {
  region = "us-east-1"
}


module "web_instance" {
  source       = "./modules/ec2_instance"
  ami          = "ami-0c55b159cbfafe1f0"
  instance_type = "t2.small"
  name         = "web-terraform"
  environment  = "dev"
}
```

outputs.tf:

lua

```
output "web_ip" {
  value = module.web_instance.instance_ip
}
```

By running terraform init, terraform plan, and terraform apply, Terraform will create an EC2 instance using the module and display the public IP in the output. The same module can be reused in another project or to create multiple instances with different configurations.

Common Error Resolution

Error: Invalid module path in source parameter.
Solution: Check if the local path is correct and accessible. For remote modules, review the URL, subdirectory formatting, and authentication.

Error: Expected variable not assigned in module block.
Solution: Check the module's variables.tf and provide all required parameters in the module block.

Error: Module output cannot be resolved.
Solution: Confirm that the output is correctly declared in the module's outputs.tf. Also check if the reference module.<name>.<output> is correct.

Error: Resource name collision inside reused module.
Solution: Keep generic names inside the module and avoid hardcoding. Use variables for names and tags.

Error: Unexpected resource update when reusing module.
Solution: Control module versions with stable commits or releases. Never reference the main branch directly in production.

Error: Lack of consistency between projects when reusing manually copied module.
Solution: Centralize modules in remote and versioned repositories. Avoid code duplication.

Best Practices

- Create small, cohesive modules specialized in a single function.

- Always define variables with description, type, and default values when appropriate.

- Use outputs to expose only what's necessary, maintaining

encapsulation.

- Prefer versioned modules stored in Git repositories or the Terraform Registry.

- Document each module with a README.md explaining usage, inputs, outputs, and examples.

- Validate and test modules before releasing new versions.

- Control versions with Git tags; never reference main directly.

- Use terraform-docs to generate automated module documentation.

- Standardize the module structure with main.tf, variables.tf, outputs.tf, and README.md.

- Maintain a central module repository in the organization, promoting reuse and governance.

Strategic Summary

The use of modules in Terraform is one of the most effective practices to scale infrastructure with quality and consistency. They encapsulate recurring logic, promote safe reuse, and allow you to apply technical standards broadly across the organization. By separating resource logic into modules, teams gain agility, reduce manual errors, and facilitate continuous infrastructure maintenance.

Creating modules requires discipline in defining variables, outputs, and file structure. When well implemented, they can be reused across multiple projects and environments without changing a single line of code. Integration with Git repositories and the use of versioning further strengthens change control, allowing controlled and predictable updates.

Common errors — such as incorrect paths, missing variables, invalid outputs, and name conflicts — can be avoided with rigorous validation, standardization, and development best practices. Module documentation is as important as its code: it ensures that other teams can use them correctly and contributes to the scalability of operations.

Modules not only increase efficiency but also reinforce governance and technical quality in infrastructure as code. They create a shared mental model among teams, promote a culture of reuse, and align operations with modern engineering principles.

CHAPTER 7. STATE MANAGEMENT

State management in Terraform is one of the fundamental pillars to ensure the integrity, traceability, and predictability of infrastructure-as-code operations. The state is the heart of Terraform: it stores all information about the managed resources, allowing the tool to know what has been created, changed, or destroyed, and to calculate the next actions to execute. Without proper state management, Terraform projects risk inconsistency, environment corruption, change overlap, and even loss of critical infrastructure. In this module, we will deeply explore the difference between local state and remote state, understand the role of backends and locking, discuss security practices to protect the state, identify common errors, and present best practices for safe and scalable operation. We will finish with a strategic summary connecting all these points.

Local State vs. Remote State

By default, Terraform stores the state in a file called terraform.tfstate, located in the working directory where the commands are run. This is known as local state. It works well for local tests, small projects, or individual experimentation, but has several limitations as the project grows.

Local State:

Advantages:

- Simple to configure.

- Quick to test small code snippets.

- No external dependencies.

Disadvantages:

- Vulnerable to data loss (disk failure, accidental deletion, corruption).

- No locking to prevent concurrency (two users can overwrite the file simultaneously).

- Difficult collaboration in teams.

- Stores sensitive information on the local disk.

Remote State:

Remote state stores the state file in a remote backend, such as Amazon S3, Azure Blob Storage, Google Cloud Storage, Terraform Cloud, Consul, among others. It is essential for collaborative projects because it enables secure state sharing among team members and provides locking mechanisms to prevent simultaneous changes.

Advantages:

- Enables collaboration among multiple users.

- Supports locking to prevent simultaneous changes.

- Facilitates backups and disaster recovery.

- Can be protected with encryption and access policies.

Disadvantages:

- Requires additional configuration.

- Depends on external infrastructure.

- May incur operational costs depending on the backend.

In professional teams and production environments, using remote state is not just recommended — it is mandatory to ensure integrity and governance.

Backends and Locking

The backend in Terraform is the mechanism responsible for storing and managing the state. It also defines how operations are executed and where outputs are saved. Among the most popular backends are:

- Amazon S3 + DynamoDB → A consolidated standard in the AWS world. S3 stores the terraform.tfstate file, while DynamoDB provides locking to prevent simultaneous changes.

- Azure Blob Storage → Stores the state in Azure and supports native locking.

- Google Cloud Storage (GCS) → Google Cloud backend that offers encryption and detailed access control.

- Terraform Cloud → HashiCorp's official service, providing state storage, remote execution, and advanced collaboration.

- Consul → Distributed backend mainly used in multi-region and on-premises architectures.

Example configuration using S3 with locking on DynamoDB:

nginx

```
terraform {
  backend "s3" {
    bucket       = "my-terraform-state"
    key          = "prod/terraform.tfstate"
    region       = "us-east-1"
    dynamodb_table = "terraform-lock"
    encrypt      = true
  }
}
```

Locking prevents multiple users from applying changes simultaneously, preventing state corruption. When a user runs terraform apply, a lock is acquired; meanwhile, other users trying to modify the same backend will see messages informing that the state is locked and will need to wait or cancel their operations.

Without locking, infrastructure is at risk of being overwritten, duplicated, or incorrectly deleted, potentially causing financial costs and serious operational impacts.

State Security

The terraform.tfstate file stores detailed information about the infrastructure, including resource IDs, endpoints, private keys, passwords, tokens, and other sensitive data. Therefore, its security must be treated as a priority.

Fundamental practices to protect the state:

- Encryption → Enable encryption in the backend. S3, Azure Blob Storage, and GCS offer native encryption. In Terraform Cloud, it is already enabled by default.

- Access control (IAM) → Restrict who can read and write in the backend. Use granular policies, granting minimal necessary permissions.

- Avoid local versioning → Do not commit terraform.tfstate files to Git repositories. Add terraform.tfstate and *.tfstate.backup to .gitignore.

- Backup routine → Configure automatic backups in the backend to allow recovery in case of failures.

- Sensitive outputs → Mark confidential outputs with sensitive = true so they are not displayed in the terminal or stored in CI/CD pipelines.

- Audit and monitoring → Enable access logs in the backend to track who accessed or modified the state.

Common Error Resolution

Error: terraform.tfstate file not found.
Solution: Check if the backend was properly initialized with terraform init and if the access credentials are configured.

Error: Active state lock preventing changes.
Solution: Wait for automatic unlock after the active operation, or use terraform force-unlock <LOCK_ID> with caution, ensuring no operations are in progress.

Error: Conflict between local and remote state.
Solution: Run terraform init -reconfigure to realign the configuration and synchronize the backend.

Error: Permission denied on remote backend.
Solution: Review credentials, roles, and policies in the backend

service. Ensure the current user or role has read and write access.

Error: Corruption of the state file.
Solution: Restore an available backup in the backend. In backends like S3, use versioning to revert to the last stable version.

Error: Sensitive outputs displayed in the terminal.
Solution: Add sensitive = true in the sensitive outputs blocks to avoid exposure.

Best Practices

- Always use remote state in production projects.

- Configure locking in the backend to avoid simultaneous changes.

- Enable encryption in the backend and never store unprotected state.

- Manage access permissions to the state granularly.

- Do not version the state in Git; protect these files with .gitignore.

- Split the state into workspaces or multiple backends when handling environments (dev, staging, prod).

- Perform regular backups and test recovery processes.

- Document the backend configuration in the repository to align the team.

- Use terraform show cautiously, as it displays the full state content.

- Integrate the state into CI/CD pipelines securely, avoiding leakage of confidential information.

Strategic Summary

State management in Terraform is a strategic component that directly impacts the stability and security of infrastructure operations. Understanding the difference between local and remote state allows you to make choices aligned with the project's size and criticality. While local state is suitable only for testing and initial development, remote state with locking and encryption is essential for collaborative and production environments.

The backends available in the Terraform ecosystem provide flexibility to integrate state management into existing infrastructure, ensuring reliability, traceability, and access control. Using locking mechanisms is an indispensable practice to avoid concurrency conflicts that could corrupt the environment.

The security of the state should be treated with the same priority given to the security of passwords and private keys. The terraform.tfstate file contains sensitive information that, if exposed, can compromise not only technical resources but also organizational reputation and security.

CHAPTER 8. INTEGRATION WITH AWS

The integration of Terraform with AWS begins with the proper configuration of the provider, which acts as the link between Terraform and AWS services. The AWS provider is responsible for translating Terraform's declarative instructions into API calls understood by AWS, enabling the creation, update, and destruction of cloud resources.

First, it's necessary to add the provider block in the Terraform configuration file, usually called main.tf. This block specifies which provider will be used and defines essential parameters such as the region. A basic example is:

hcl

```
provider "aws" {
  region = "us-east-1"
}
```

In addition, it's recommended to manage AWS credentials securely. Credentials can be provided through environment variables, configuration files (~/.aws/credentials), or profiles configured with the AWS CLI. An example using a profile would be:

hcl

```
provider "aws" {
```

```hcl
  profile = "default"

  region  = "us-east-1"

}
```

The provider version should also be specified in the versions.tf file to ensure compatibility and execution stability:

hcl

```hcl
terraform {

  required_providers {

    aws = {

      source  = "hashicorp/aws"

      version = "~> 5.0"

    }

  }

}
```

This approach prevents surprises from unexpected API changes between versions.

Deploying EC2, S3, RDS

Once the provider is properly configured, the next step is to deploy AWS services with Terraform, such as EC2, S3, and RDS.

EC2

Creating an EC2 instance involves specifying the AMI (Amazon Machine Image), instance type, and additional configurations such as key pair, security groups, and subnet. Example configuration:

hcl

```
resource "aws_instance" "web" {
  ami           = "ami-0c55b159cbfafe1f0"
  instance_type = "t2.micro"

  tags = {
    Name = "TerraformEC2"
  }
}
```

This code provisions a basic instance. For more robust environments, it's important to define security groups, load balancers, and appropriate roles.

S3

S3 allows for object storage, such as files and images. Deploying an S3 bucket with Terraform is simple:

hcl

```
resource "aws_s3_bucket" "bucket" {
  bucket = "my-terraform-bucket"
  acl    = "private"
}
```

Other configurations, such as versioning, encryption, and access policies, can be added to meet specific security and compliance demands.

RDS

Deploying an RDS database requires special attention, as it involves not only creating the database but also defining the

engine, version, instance, master user, and network parameters:
hcl

```
resource "aws_db_instance" "default" {
  allocated_storage   = 20
  engine          = "mysql"
  engine_version     = "8.0"
  instance_class     = "db.t2.micro"
  name          = "mydatabase"
  username        = "admin"
  password        = "securepassword123"
  parameter_group_name = "default.mysql8.0"
}
```

It's critical not to expose sensitive credentials directly in the code. Use terraform.tfvars or a secrets manager to store them securely.

Secure Authentication

Ensuring secure authentication between Terraform and AWS is a mandatory practice. The most common approaches include:

- **Use of environment variables:** set AWS_ACCESS_KEY_ID and AWS_SECRET_ACCESS_KEY in the system environment.

- **Use of AWS CLI profiles:** configure in the ~/.aws/ credentials file and reference in the provider.

- **IAM Roles:** when running Terraform on EC2 or managed services, assign roles to the instance, avoiding explicit credentials.

- **Vault/Secrets Manager:** store sensitive credentials in secret vaults and inject them dynamically into the environment.

Also, enable MFA for human users and minimize credential exposure when using CI/CD pipelines. Tools like aws-vault help manage temporary credentials with reinforced security.

Common Error Resolution

During the integration of Terraform with AWS, various errors can occur. Below are typical errors and their solutions:

Error: InvalidClientTokenId
Cause: Incorrect or missing credentials.
Solution: Check the credentials file, AWS profile, and environment variables. Run aws configure to fix.

Error: UnauthorizedOperation
Cause: Insufficient IAM permissions.
Solution: Ensure that the user or role has appropriate policies (such as AmazonEC2FullAccess, AmazonS3FullAccess).

Error: RequestLimitExceeded
Cause: API limit reached.
Solution: Increase the limit with AWS or add depends_on and time_sleep between resources making many requests.

Error: terraform plan does not recognize state changes
Cause: Corrupted or divergent remote state.
Solution: Run terraform refresh or recreate the backend. In critical cases, use terraform state for manual fixes.

Error: Error creating DB Instance
Cause: Incompatible RDS parameters (engine, version, storage).
Solution: Consult AWS documentation to validate supported combinations.

The key to effective error resolution lies in carefully reading Terraform logs and AWS error messages, and enabling TF_LOG=DEBUG when necessary.

Best Practices

Integrating Terraform with AWS requires adopting best practices to ensure security, scalability, and maintainability.

- **Modularization:** Organize resources into reusable modules for EC2, S3, RDS, and other services.

- **Remote backend:** Use S3 with DynamoDB to store the remote state, ensuring team consistency.

- **Versioning:** Lock provider and module versions to prevent updates from breaking infrastructure.

- **Environment separation:** Use workspaces or separate files for dev, staging, and prod environments.

- **Encryption:** Always enable encryption for S3 and RDS.

- **Tags:** Add consistent tags to identify resources and facilitate management and billing.

- **Least privilege policy:** Configure IAM policies that grant only strictly necessary permissions.

- **Auditing:** Enable CloudTrail to log all changes made in AWS, including those from Terraform.

Additionally, perform periodic Terraform code reviews with peers or through automated pipelines, validating changes before applying them in production.

Strategic Summary

Integrating Terraform with AWS represents a leap in efficiency for infrastructure management, enabling automation from configuring VMs, buckets, and databases to governing access and security policies. The AWS provider configuration is the first critical step and should be done with special attention to credentials, regions, and versions.

Deploying resources such as EC2, S3, and RDS demonstrates Terraform's flexibility in handling multiple services but requires special attention to resource dependencies and state management. Secure authentication is a non-negotiable layer, as key and credential leaks can compromise the entire environment.

Common errors, when well understood, cease to be obstacles and become milestones of operational learning and maturity. They highlight the importance of understanding Terraform and AWS messages, as well as the need for good monitoring.

Finally, adopting best practices such as modularization, use of remote backend, environment separation, encryption, and auditing not only ensures environment stability but also the scalability of operations, making the team more agile and efficient.

The practical application of these strategies enables the delivery of infrastructure as code with reliability, replicability, and security, maximizing the engineering team's potential and generating sustainable competitive advantage.

CHAPTER 9. INTEGRATION WITH AZURE

The integration between Terraform and Microsoft Azure is one of the most powerful combinations for professionals looking to provision and manage infrastructure in an automated, secure, and scalable manner. Terraform acts as an intermediary between the user's declarative code and Azure resources, translating instructions into API calls and ensuring the infrastructure state remains aligned with the desired configuration. In this chapter, we will detail how to configure the Azure provider, deploy resources such as virtual machines (VMs), Blob Storage, and SQL databases, cover key management, resolve common errors, and present best practices to ensure operational stability and security. We will conclude with a strategic summary connecting the lessons to modern professional practice.

Provider Configuration

The first step to operate with Azure using Terraform is the correct configuration of the provider. Terraform officially supports the azurerm provider, which interacts with platform services via Azure Resource Manager (ARM).

Before starting, it's essential to have an Azure account, along with the Azure CLI installed and authenticated. The following command allows you to authenticate your session:

bash

```
az login
```

After authentication, the provider block must be configured in the main .tf file:

h

```
provider "azurerm" {
  features {}
}
```

Starting from version 2.x, azurerm explicitly requires the declaration of features {} to enable desired resources. For environments with multiple subscriptions, you can explicitly specify the subscription to use:

hcl

```
provider "azurerm" {
  subscription_id = "00000000-0000-0000-0000-000000000000"
  client_id     = var.client_id
  client_secret = var.client_secret
  tenant_id     = var.tenant_id
  features {}
}
```

These parameters can be securely stored in .tfvars files or injected via environment variables. For secure and scalable operation, it's highly recommended to use Azure Service Principals with specific permissions, preferably scoped by resource group or subscription.

Deploying VMs, Blob Storage, SQL

Once the provider is configured, it's possible to provision various resources on Azure. Let's explore three of the most commonly used in corporate environments: virtual machines, Blob Storage, and SQL databases.

Virtual Machines (VMs)

Provisioning a VM on Azure involves multiple interconnected resources: resource group, virtual network, subnet, network interface, and finally, the VM itself. A basic example includes:

hcl

```
resource "azurerm_resource_group" "rg" {
  name     = "rg-tf-vm"
  location = "East US"
}


resource "azurerm_virtual_network" "vnet" {
  name            = "vnet-tf"
  address_space   = ["10.0.0.0/16"]
  location        = azurerm_resource_group.rg.location
  resource_group_name = azurerm_resource_group.rg.name
}


resource "azurerm_subnet" "subnet" {
  name            = "subnet-tf"
  resource_group_name = azurerm_resource_group.rg.name
  virtual_network_name =
azurerm_virtual_network.vnet.name
```

```
  address_prefixes   = ["10.0.1.0/24"]
}


resource "azurerm_network_interface" "nic" {
  name          = "nic-tf"
  location        = azurerm_resource_group.rg.location
  resource_group_name = azurerm_resource_group.rg.name

  ip_configuration {
    name              = "internal"
    subnet_id               = azurerm_subnet.subnet.id
    private_ip_address_allocation = "Dynamic"
  }
}


resource "azurerm_linux_virtual_machine" "vm" {
  name          = "vm-tf"
  resource_group_name  = azurerm_resource_group.rg.name
  location         = azurerm_resource_group.rg.location
  size        = "Standard_B1s"
  admin_username     = "adminuser"
  network_interface_ids = [azurerm_network_interface.nic.id]

  admin_ssh_key {
    username  = "adminuser"
```

```hcl
  public_key = file("~/.ssh/id_rsa.pub")
}


os_disk {
  caching        = "ReadWrite"
  storage_account_type = "Standard_LRS"
}


source_image_reference {
  publisher = "Canonical"
  offer   = "UbuntuServer"
  sku     = "20_04-lts"
  version  = "latest"
 }
}
```

Blob Storage

The Blob Storage service is used to store files, images, backups, and binary objects in the cloud. A simple creation example:

hcl

```hcl
resource "azurerm_storage_account" "sa" {
  name            = "storagetfexample"
  resource_group_name   = azurerm_resource_group.rg.name
  location         = azurerm_resource_group.rg.location
  account_tier      = "Standard"
```

```hcl
  account_replication_type = "LRS"
}


resource "azurerm_storage_container" "container" {
  name             = "myfiles"
  storage_account_name = azurerm_storage_account.sa.name
  container_access_type = "private"
}
```

SQL Database

Provisioning an SQL database involves creating the server and the database instance itself:

hcl

```hcl
resource "azurerm_sql_server" "sql" {
  name                 = "sqlserverterraform"
  resource_group_name       = azurerm_resource_group.rg.name
  location             = azurerm_resource_group.rg.location
  version              = "12.0"
  administrator_login      = "adminuser"
  administrator_login_password = var.db_password
}


resource "azurerm_sql_database" "database" {
  name         = "terraformdb"
  resource_group_name = azurerm_resource_group.rg.name
```

```
  location       = azurerm_resource_group.rg.location
  server_name    = azurerm_sql_server.sql.name
  sku_name       = "Basic"
}
```

Key Management

Handling credentials and sensitive data in Azure must be done securely. Terraform allows integration with resources like Azure Key Vault to store passwords, SSH keys, tokens, and connection strings with encryption and controlled access.

Example of creating a key vault:

hcl

```
resource "azurerm_key_vault" "vault" {
  name                     = "vault-tf"
  location                 = azurerm_resource_group.rg.location
  resource_group_name      = azurerm_resource_group.rg.name
  tenant_id                = var.tenant_id
  sku_name                 = "standard"
  soft_delete_enabled      = true
  purge_protection_enabled = true
}


resource "azurerm_key_vault_secret" "secret" {
  name         = "dbPassword"
  value        = var.db_password
  key_vault_id = azurerm_key_vault.vault.id
```

```
}
```

To consume the secret in a script:

hcl

```hcl
data "azurerm_key_vault_secret" "password" {
  name       = "dbPassword"
  key_vault_id = azurerm_key_vault.vault.id
}


output "db_password" {
  value    = data.azurerm_key_vault_secret.password.value
  sensitive = true
}
```

This ensures that sensitive information is not hardcoded in the code, reducing the risk of leaks.

Common Error Resolution

Error: Authentication failed: AADSTS7000215
Cause: Incorrect credentials or invalid app registration.
Solution: Check client_id, client_secret, and tenant_id. Confirm the app is properly registered in Azure AD.

Error: The Resource group was not found
Cause: Incorrect resource group reference.
Solution: Ensure the resource group was actually created before being referenced.

Error: Resource already exists

Cause: Attempt to recreate an already manually provisioned resource.
Solution: Import the existing resource with terraform import or adjust the naming strategy.

Error: No features block specified in provider configuration
Cause: Starting from version 2.0, features {} is mandatory.
Solution: Add features {} to the provider block.

Error: Insufficient privileges to access Key Vault
Cause: Insufficient permission to access the vault.
Solution: Grant Key Vault Secrets User to the identity used by the Terraform execution.

Best Practices

- Use .tfvars files to manage environment-specific configurations.

- Store passwords and secrets exclusively in Azure Key Vault.

- Modularize VM, storage, and SQL creation into reusable blocks.

- Never store credentials directly in the code.

- Use sensitive = true for all sensitive outputs.

- Enable encryption on all compatible resources.

- Use the Azure Resource Naming Standard for consistency.

- Configure logging and monitoring with Azure Monitor and Log Analytics.

- Separate environments using workspaces or distinct

directories.

- Automate plan application with CI/CD pipelines using Azure DevOps, GitHub Actions, or similar.

Strategic Summary

Integration with Azure through Terraform enables the construction of a solid, auditable, and scalable infrastructure with a high level of automation and control. Proper provider configuration, combined with a good module structure and security practices, forms the backbone of a reliable operation. Provisioning VMs, Blob Storage, and SQL databases covers the central needs of storage, processing, and data persistence for most modern applications.

Key management via Key Vault elevates operational security and positions the organization to meet compliance and governance requirements. Common errors, when well understood, can be anticipated, diagnosed, and resolved quickly.

By applying best practices such as modularization, environment segregation, sensitive output control, and pipeline automation, professionals can transform simple scripts into stable, sustainable operations aligned with the demands of large corporate environments.

CHAPTER 10. INTEGRATION WITH GOOGLE CLOUD

The integration of Terraform with Google Cloud Platform (GCP) allows you to create, manage, and scale cloud infrastructure in a highly automated and replicable manner. Terraform, acting as an infrastructure as code tool, makes the provisioning of resources like Compute Engine, Cloud Storage, and BigQuery secure and predictable, with precise control over versions and changes. This chapter details how to configure the Google Cloud provider, deploy key services, authenticate securely using service accounts, as well as address common errors, best practices, and a strategic summary to ensure operational excellence.

Provider Configuration

The first step to use Terraform with Google Cloud is to properly configure the provider. Terraform uses the google provider to connect to GCP, and it's necessary to specify the project, region, and appropriate authentication.

First, ensure that you have:

- An active Google Cloud account.

- A project created in the Console.

- The Compute Engine API enabled.

- A service account key generated.

The basic configuration in Terraform looks like this:

hcl

```
provider "google" {
  credentials = file("<PATH-TO-JSON-KEY>")
  project    = "<PROJECT-ID>"
  region     = "us-central1"
}
```

This block should be included in the main .tf file, and it's recommended that the JSON key is not stored in the repository but kept securely in the local environment, using environment variables or secret vaults.

Example configuration with variables:

hcl

```
variable "project_id" {}
variable "region" {}


provider "google" {
  project    = var.project_id
  region     = var.region
}
```

Deploying Compute Engine, Cloud Storage, BigQuery

With the provider configured, the next step is to provision resources. We will cover three of the most important in the Google Cloud ecosystem.

Compute Engine

Compute Engine allows you to create and manage virtual machines in the cloud. A basic deployment example:

hcl

```
resource "google_compute_instance" "default" {
  name         = "instance-terraform"
  machine_type = "e2-micro"
  zone         = "us-central1-a"

  boot_disk {
    initialize_params {
      image = "debian-cloud/debian-11"
    }
  }

  network_interface {
    network = "default"
    access_config {}
  }
}
```

This code creates a Debian VM with the e2-micro machine type, ideal for tests and lightweight workloads.

Cloud Storage

Cloud Storage is used to store objects and files. A bucket can be deployed as follows:

hcl

```
resource "google_storage_bucket" "bucket" {
  name        = "my-terraform-bucket"
  location    = "US"
  storage_class = "STANDARD"
}
```

For versioning control and policies, add parameters like versioning and lifecycle_rule.

BigQuery

BigQuery is a fully managed data warehouse. A basic example of creating a dataset:

hcl

```
resource "google_bigquery_dataset" "dataset" {
  dataset_id = "my_dataset"
  location  = "US"
}
```

To create a table within the dataset:

hcl

```
resource "google_bigquery_table" "table" {
  dataset_id = google_bigquery_dataset.dataset.dataset_id
  table_id  = "my_table"
  schema    = file("schema.json")
}
```

The schema.json file must contain the table schema in JSON format.

Authentication via Service Account

Authentication on Google Cloud with Terraform should preferably be done via service account. This approach ensures greater security, permission isolation, and adherence to GCP best practices.

Steps to configure:

- Create a service account in the Console.

- Grant the minimum necessary roles (e.g., Compute Admin, Storage Admin, BigQuery Admin).

- Generate and download the JSON key file.

- Configure Terraform to use the key:

bash

```bash
export GOOGLE_APPLICATION_CREDENTIALS="/path/to/key.json"
```

Or in the provider:

hcl

```hcl
provider "google" {
  credentials = file("/path/to/key.json")
  project     = var.project_id
  region      = var.region
}
```

This configuration allows Terraform to authenticate automatically in any script or CI/CD pipeline without exposing passwords or tokens in the code.

Common Error Resolution

Error: Error loading credentials from file
Cause: Incorrect JSON file path or insufficient file permissions.
Solution: Confirm the absolute system path and adjust permissions with chmod 600.

Error: 403 The caller does not have permission
Cause: Service account without sufficient permissions for the resource.
Solution: Assign the appropriate roles to the account, avoiding excessive permissions.

Error: Error 409: Already Exists
Cause: Attempt to create a resource that already exists.
Solution: Change the resource name or import it with terraform import into the state.

Error: Invalid value for field 'resource.name'
Cause: Invalid name or name not complying with Google Cloud restrictions.
Solution: Use names compatible with service naming rules, usually lowercase and without special characters.

Error: Timeout while waiting for operation to complete
Cause: Resource provisioning taking longer than the default limit.
Solution: Increase timeouts using timeouts blocks or review the cause of the delay.

Error: Cannot find default VPC
Cause: GCP account without a default network created.

Solution: Manually create the default network or explicitly define networks and subnets in Terraform.

Best Practices

Adopting best practices when using Terraform with Google Cloud is essential to avoid errors, reduce costs, and ensure security.

- Modularize resources using reusable blocks for Compute Engine, Storage, and BigQuery.

- Use workspaces or directory separation to isolate environments (dev, stage, prod).

- Manage credentials securely, never storing JSON files in the repository.

- Enable versioning in Cloud Storage to prevent accidental data loss.

- Assign the minimum necessary permissions to the service account to reduce the attack surface.

- Mark confidential outputs with sensitive = true to avoid exposure in logs.

- Implement audit routines with Stackdriver Logging and Cloud Audit Logs.

- Use terraform fmt and terraform validate to ensure code readability and integrity.

- Configure remote backends, such as Google Cloud Storage, to securely store state and enable team collaboration.

- Automate executions with CI/CD pipelines in Cloud Build,

GitHub Actions, or GitLab CI.

Strategic Summary

Integrating Terraform with Google Cloud significantly expands the engineering team's capacity by enabling declarative and versioned infrastructure provisioning and management. The provider configuration and authentication via service account form the foundation of secure operations, while deploying resources such as Compute Engine, Cloud Storage, and BigQuery covers core processing, storage, and data analysis needs.

Careful credential management, combined with disciplined best practice use, ensures security, compliance, and operational efficiency. Common errors, although frequent, can be resolved quickly when the team understands their causes and adopts continuous validation processes.

The consistent application of these strategies transforms Terraform into a catalyst for robust, auditable, and scalable operations on Google Cloud. In addition to reducing manual errors, proper use of Terraform saves time and costs, promotes team collaboration, and strengthens IT governance.

CHAPTER 11. NETWORK PROVISIONING

Provisioning networks with Terraform is one of the most critical steps to ensure scalable, secure, and highly available environments. By mastering the creation of VPCs, subnets, firewall rules, load balancers, and even cross-cloud configurations, professionals expand their ability to deliver modern and resilient solutions. This chapter details how to perform network provisioning, integrate multiple clouds, configure load balancing, handle common errors, and apply best practices to ensure consistency, performance, and security.

VPC, Subnets, Firewall Rules

The foundation of any modern network starts with creating a Virtual Private Cloud (VPC), which defines an isolated IP address space where resources such as VMs, databases, and containers are deployed. The VPC enables the separation of internal and external traffic, the application of specific firewall rules, and the efficient organization of applications.

Example on AWS:

hcl

```
resource "aws_vpc" "main" {
  cidr_block = "10.0.0.0/16"
  enable_dns_support   = true
  enable_dns_hostnames = true
  tags = {
```

```
    Name = "main-vpc"
  }
}


resource "aws_subnet" "subnet1" {
  vpc_id   = aws_vpc.main.id
  cidr_block = "10.0.1.0/24"
  availability_zone = "us-east-1a"
  tags = {
    Name = "subnet-1"
  }
}


resource "aws_security_group" "allow_http" {
  vpc_id = aws_vpc.main.id
  ingress {
    from_port  = 80
    to_port    = 80
    protocol   = "tcp"
    cidr_blocks = ["0.0.0.0/0"]
  }
  egress {
    from_port  = 0
    to_port    = 0
    protocol   = "-1"
```

```hcl
    cidr_blocks = ["0.0.0.0/0"]
  }
}
```

On Google Cloud:

hcl

```hcl
resource "google_compute_network" "vpc_network" {
  name = "vpc-network"
}


resource "google_compute_subnetwork" "subnet" {
  name          = "subnet"
  ip_cidr_range = "10.0.1.0/24"
  region        = "us-central1"
  network       = google_compute_network.vpc_network.self_link
}


resource "google_compute_firewall" "allow-http" {
  name    = "allow-http"
  network = google_compute_network.vpc_network.name

  allow {
    protocol = "tcp"
    ports    = ["80"]
  }
```

```hcl
  source_ranges = ["0.0.0.0/0"]
}
```

On Azure:

hcl

```hcl
resource "azurerm_virtual_network" "vnet" {
  name              = "vnet"
  address_space     = ["10.0.0.0/16"]
  location          = azurerm_resource_group.rg.location
  resource_group_name = azurerm_resource_group.rg.name
}


resource "azurerm_subnet" "subnet" {
  name              = "subnet"
  resource_group_name = azurerm_resource_group.rg.name
  virtual_network_name =
azurerm_virtual_network.vnet.name
  address_prefixes  = ["10.0.1.0/24"]
}


resource "azurerm_network_security_group" "nsg" {
  name              = "nsg"
  location          = azurerm_resource_group.rg.location
  resource_group_name = azurerm_resource_group.rg.name
```

```
security_rule {

    name              = "Allow-HTTP"

    priority          = 100

    direction         = "Inbound"

    access            = "Allow"

    protocol          = "Tcp"

    source_port_range        = "*"

    destination_port_range   = "80"

    source_address_prefix    = "*"

    destination_address_prefix = "*"

  }

}
```

These examples illustrate how to define the fundamental layer of the network: the VPC, subnets, and firewall rules, ensuring isolation, security, and efficient routing.

Cross-Cloud Configuration

Cross-cloud provisioning refers to the ability to interconnect networks across different providers, such as AWS, Azure, and Google Cloud, creating hybrid or multi-cloud architectures. This practice is adopted by organizations seeking to avoid lock-in, increase resilience, or distribute workloads across geographic regions.

Several approaches can connect different clouds:

- **Site-to-Site VPN:** connects VPCs from distinct providers using VPN gateways.

- **Cross-cloud Peering:** connects networks via native peering, where supported.

- **SD-WAN or third-party solutions:** uses virtual appliances to orchestrate and manage multi-cloud connectivity.

Example of VPN configuration on AWS:

hcl

```
resource "aws_vpn_gateway" "vpn_gw" {
  vpc_id = aws_vpc.main.id
}


resource "aws_customer_gateway" "customer_gw" {
  bgp_asn    = 65000
  ip_address = "1.2.3.4"
  type       = "ipsec.1"
}


resource "aws_vpn_connection" "vpn_conn" {
  vpn_gateway_id     = aws_vpn_gateway.vpn_gw.id
  customer_gateway_id =
aws_customer_gateway.customer_gw.id
  type          = "ipsec.1"
}
```

Cross-cloud configuration requires special attention to latency, security, and costs. It is essential to design clear routing policies, monitor traffic, and apply end-to-end encryption.

Load Balancing

Load balancing distributes traffic across multiple servers to ensure high availability and performance. With Terraform, you can provision load balancers on all major providers.

Example on AWS (Elastic Load Balancer):

hcl

```
resource "aws_lb" "app_lb" {
  name               = "app-lb"
  internal           = false
  load_balancer_type = "application"
  subnets            = [aws_subnet.subnet1.id]

  enable_deletion_protection = false
}


resource "aws_lb_target_group" "app_tg" {
  name     = "app-tg"
  port     = 80
  protocol = "HTTP"
  vpc_id   = aws_vpc.main.id
}


resource "aws_lb_listener" "front_end" {
  load_balancer_arn = aws_lb.app_lb.arn
  port              = "80"
```

```hcl
  protocol      = "HTTP"


  default_action {
    type       = "forward"
    target_group_arn = aws_lb_target_group.app_tg.arn
  }
}
```

On Google Cloud:

hcl

```hcl
resource "google_compute_forwarding_rule" "default" {
  name            = "forwarding-rule"
  load_balancing_scheme = "EXTERNAL"
  port_range      = "80"
  target          = google_compute_target_pool.default.self_link
}
```

On Azure:

hcl

```hcl
resource "azurerm_lb" "lb" {
  name         = "example-lb"
  location     = azurerm_resource_group.rg.location
  resource_group_name = azurerm_resource_group.rg.name
  frontend_ip_configuration {
    name              = "PublicIPAddress"
```

```
  public_ip_address_id     = azurerm_public_ip.lb_public_ip.id
}
}
```

Proper load balancing improves resilience and distributes requests efficiently, reducing overload risk.

Common Error Resolution

Error: CIDR block overlapping
Cause: Overlapping IP ranges between VPCs or subnets.
Solution: Carefully plan the IP space to avoid conflicts and validate ranges before deployment.

Error: Port conflict in firewall rules
Cause: Two conflicting rules for the same port.
Solution: Adjust rules to ensure only one takes precedence or combine rules into a single block.

Error: Failed VPN connection establishment
Cause: Incorrect tunnel, BGP, or IP configuration.
Solution: Review configuration parameters, confirm credentials, and test connectivity with tools like ping and traceroute.

Error: Target group not registered with load balancer
Cause: Missing association between instances and target group.
Solution: Ensure instances are properly associated and explicitly register them.

Error: Route not propagating
Cause: Missing route configuration between VPCs, subnets, or gateways.
Solution: Add routes manually or configure dynamic propagation in VPN and peering.

Best Practices

- Plan and document the IP scheme before provisioning to avoid overlap.

- Use consistent tags to identify network resources.

- Separate subnets by traffic type (public/private) to improve security.

- Enable flow logs to monitor traffic and diagnose issues.

- Use modules to standardize network creation across environments.

- Automate connectivity tests after deployment using scripts integrated into the pipeline.

- Enable high availability on load balancers and gateways.

- Implement firewall rules following the principle of least privilege.

- Set up alerts and monitoring for network events.

- Periodically review and clean up unused rules and routes.

Strategic Summary

Provisioning networks with Terraform is essential for any modern architecture seeking scalability, security, and resilience. Creating VPCs, subnets, and firewall rules establishes the foundation of an isolated and controlled environment. Load balancing ensures efficient traffic distribution and guarantees high availability.

Cross-cloud configurations extend the boundaries of infrastructure, enabling integration between different providers and offering strategic flexibility for businesses seeking redundancy and global optimization. Mastering network provisioning turns professionals into strategic assets capable of designing and delivering complex infrastructures with quality and predictability.

CHAPTER 12. STORAGE PROVISIONING

Storage provisioning with Terraform is one of the most important elements to support modern workloads, whether for computing, databases, analytics, backups, or disaster recovery. Well-planned storage ensures not only performance but also security, redundancy, and proper governance. In this chapter, we will explore how to provision buckets, volumes, and snapshots across major providers, configure access policies, present multi-cloud examples, analyze common errors, share best practices, and conclude with a strategic summary that connects everything to professional operations.

Buckets, Volumes, Snapshots

Each provider offers different storage resources that meet various project needs. Terraform allows you to manage all of them uniformly and consistently.

AWS

Buckets with S3

h

```
resource "aws_s3_bucket" "meu_bucket" {
  bucket = "meu-bucket-terraform"
  acl   = "private"
}
```

Volumes with EBS

hcl

```
resource "aws_ebs_volume" "meu_volume" {
  availability_zone = "us-east-1a"
  size        = 20
  type        = "gp2"
}
```

Snapshots

hcl

```
resource "aws_ebs_snapshot" "meu_snapshot" {
  volume_id = aws_ebs_volume.meu_volume.id
  description = "Backup do volume de dados"
}
```

Google Cloud

Buckets with Cloud Storage

hcl

```
resource "google_storage_bucket" "bucket" {
  name      = "meu-bucket-gcp"
  location   = "US"
  storage_class = "STANDARD"
}
```

Volumes with Persistent Disk

hcl

```hcl
resource "google_compute_disk" "meu_volume" {
  name = "meu-disco"
  type = "pd-standard"
  zone = "us-central1-a"
  size = 20
}
```

Snapshots

hcl

```hcl
resource "google_compute_snapshot" "meu_snapshot" {
  name        = "snapshot-disco"
  source_disk = google_compute_disk.meu_volume.id
}
```

Azure

Buckets with Blob Storage

hcl

```hcl
resource "azurerm_storage_account" "storage" {
  name                = "storagetf"
  resource_group_name = azurerm_resource_group.rg.name
  location            = azurerm_resource_group.rg.location
  account_tier        = "Standard"
```

```hcl
  account_replication_type = "LRS"
}


resource "azurerm_storage_container" "container" {
  name            = "meusarquivos"
  storage_account_name =
azurerm_storage_account.storage.name
  container_access_type = "private"
}
```

Volumes with Managed Disks

hcl

```hcl
resource "azurerm_managed_disk" "meu_volume" {
  name            = "meu-disco"
  location          = azurerm_resource_group.rg.location
  resource_group_name = azurerm_resource_group.rg.name
  storage_account_type = "Standard_LRS"
  disk_size_gb      = 20
  create_option     = "Empty"
}
```

Snapshots

hcl

```hcl
resource "azurerm_snapshot" "meu_snapshot" {
  name            = "snapshot-disco"
```

```
location        = azurerm_resource_group.rg.location
resource_group_name = azurerm_resource_group.rg.name
create_option   = "Copy"
source_uri      = azurerm_managed_disk.meu_volume.id
}
```

Access Policies

Configuring appropriate access policies ensures that only authorized users and applications can interact with storage resources.

AWS S3 Policy

hcl

```
resource "aws_s3_bucket_policy" "policy" {
  bucket = aws_s3_bucket.meu_bucket.id
  policy = jsonencode({
    Version = "2012-10-17",
    Statement = [{
      Effect = "Allow",
      Principal = "*",
      Action = ["s3:GetObject"],
      Resource = "${aws_s3_bucket.meu_bucket.arn}/*"
    }]
  })
}
```

Google Cloud IAM

hcl

```hcl
resource "google_storage_bucket_iam_member" "member" {
  bucket = google_storage_bucket.bucket.name
  role   = "roles/storage.objectViewer"
  member = "user:usuario@example.com"
}
```

Azure Role Assignment

hcl

```hcl
resource "azurerm_role_assignment" "assignment" {
  scope               = azurerm_storage_account.storage.id
  role_definition_name = "Storage Blob Data Reader"
  principal_id        =
azurerm_user_assigned_identity.identidade.principal_id
}
```

Multi-Cloud Example

In multi-cloud environments, a single Terraform configuration can orchestrate resources across AWS, Azure, and Google Cloud:

hcl

```hcl
# AWS
resource "aws_s3_bucket" "bucket_aws" {
  bucket = "multi-cloud-aws"
}
```

```
# Google Cloud
resource "google_storage_bucket" "bucket_gcp" {
  name    = "multi-cloud-gcp"
  location = "US"
}


# Azure
resource "azurerm_storage_account" "bucket_azure" {
  name                = "multicloudazure"
  resource_group_name    = azurerm_resource_group.rg.name
  location            = azurerm_resource_group.rg.location
  account_tier         = "Standard"
  account_replication_type = "LRS"
}
```

This example shows how to centralize storage management across clouds, ensuring consistency and facilitating hybrid operations.

Common Error Resolution

Error: Bucket name already exists
Cause: The global bucket name is duplicated.
Solution: Use unique names by adding dynamic prefixes or suffixes, such as ${var.project}-${random_id.suffix.hex}.

Error: Permission denied
Cause: Missing or incorrect credentials or policies.

Solution: Check roles, policies, and keys, ensuring the identity used has appropriate permissions.

Error: Resource not found
Cause: The referenced resource does not exist.
Solution: Confirm creation order, dependencies, and names used in the code.

Error: API rate limit exceeded
Cause: Excessive requests in a short period.
Solution: Add timeouts or depends_on to distribute the request load.

Error: Snapshot creation failed
Cause: The source disk is in use or locked.
Solution: Stop the resource or use consistent snapshots with the provider's native mechanisms.

Best Practices

- Use standardized and consistent names for buckets and volumes.

- Enable encryption on all storage resources.

- Configure policies using the principle of least privilege.

- Enable versioning on buckets and automatic snapshots to protect against data loss.

- Separate storage by environment (dev, staging, prod) using workspaces or .tfvars files.

- Integrate storage into backup and disaster recovery pipelines.

- Document the data retention and access policy.

- Use modules to standardize deployments across multiple providers.

- Configure logs and metrics to monitor usage and alert on anomalies.

- Automate cleanup of obsolete resources to avoid unnecessary costs.

Strategic Summary

Storage provisioning with Terraform enhances IT teams' capabilities by enabling centralized, secure, and scalable management of cloud data. Buckets, volumes, and snapshots are essential elements that, when well configured, support critical workloads, backups, and multi-cloud integrations. Access policies represent a vital layer to protect assets and ensure compliance with internal and regulatory standards.

The use of multi-cloud examples shows that Terraform not only provisions resources but also unifies operations across different providers, creating flexible and hybrid environments. Anticipating and resolving common errors helps accelerate adoption and operational maturity.

CHAPTER 13. DATABASE PROVISIONING

Provisioning databases with Terraform represents a fundamental leap for automating modern environments, allowing PostgreSQL, MySQL, and other data services to be created, configured, and maintained with consistency and reproducibility. Automating databases with Terraform reduces the risk of manual errors, accelerates the deployment of test and production environments, and ensures that backups, permissions, and access policies are aligned with best practices. This chapter details how to provision PostgreSQL and MySQL databases on major providers, configure backups, manage users and permissions, resolve common errors, and apply best practices, closing with a strategic summary that ties all these points to professional practice.

Deploying PostgreSQL, MySQL

Terraform offers resources to provision databases both at the infrastructure level (using managed cloud services) and at the configuration level, integrating external modules or specialized providers.

AWS RDS

On AWS, Amazon RDS offers managed databases for PostgreSQL and MySQL.

Example of RDS database creation for PostgreSQL:

hcl

```
resource "aws_db_instance" "postgres" {
```

```hcl
  identifier     = "postgres-tf"
  engine         = "postgres"
  engine_version = "14"
  instance_class = "db.t3.micro"
  allocated_storage = 20
  name           = "meudb"
  username       = "admin"
  password       = var.db_password
  parameter_group_name = "default.postgres14"
  skip_final_snapshot = true
}
```

For MySQL:

hcl

```hcl
resource "aws_db_instance" "mysql" {
  identifier     = "mysql-tf"
  engine         = "mysql"
  engine_version = "8.0"
  instance_class = "db.t3.micro"
  allocated_storage = 20
  name           = "meudb"
  username       = "admin"
  password       = var.db_password
  parameter_group_name = "default.mysql8.0"
  skip_final_snapshot = true
```

}

Google Cloud SQL

On Google Cloud, we use Cloud SQL:

hcl

```
resource "google_sql_database_instance" "postgres" {
  name             = "postgres-tf"
  database_version = "POSTGRES_14"
  region           = "us-central1"

  settings {
    tier = "db-f1-micro"
  }
}
```

Azure Database for PostgreSQL/MySQL

On Azure, we use Azure Database for PostgreSQL and MySQL:

hcl

```
resource "azurerm_postgresql_server" "postgres" {
  name                = "postgres-tf"
  location            = azurerm_resource_group.rg.location
  resource_group_name = azurerm_resource_group.rg.name
  administrator_login          = "adminuser"
  administrator_login_password = var.db_password
  sku_name            = "B_Gen5_1"
```

```hcl
  version        = "14"
  storage_mb       = 51200
}
```

Backup Configuration

Backups ensure data integrity and the ability to recover in case of failures. Each provider offers native options that can be configured via Terraform.

AWS RDS Backup

hcl

```hcl
backup_retention_period = 7
backup_window      = "03:00-04:00"
```

This block within the aws_db_instance resource defines that 7 days of backup will be kept, performed between 3 AM and 4 AM UTC.

Google Cloud SQL Backup

hcl

```hcl
settings {
  backup_configuration {
    enabled        = true
    start_time       = "03:00"
    point_in_time_recovery_enabled = true
  }
}
```

Azure PostgreSQL Backup

On Azure, automatic backups are enabled by default, but we can define the retention:

hcl

```
backup_retention_days = 7

geo_redundant_backup_enabled = true
```

Backup retention should always be aligned with business policy, considering compliance and recovery requirements.

Creating Users and Permissions

Although Terraform does not directly execute SQL commands inside the database, there are providers and modules that help create users and permissions.

AWS RDS

To create additional users, we typically use external scripts run after deployment, but we can manage parameters:

hcl

```
resource "aws_db_parameter_group" "postgres_params" {
  name        = "postgres-params"
  family      = "postgres14"
  description = "Custom parameters"

  parameter {
    name  = "log_statement"
    value = "all"
```

```
  }
}
```

Google Cloud SQL User

hcl

```
resource "google_sql_user" "db_user" {
  name     = "usuario"
  instance = google_sql_database_instance.postgres.name
  password = var.db_user_password
}
```

Azure Database User (via external script)

On Azure, after provisioning the database, we can connect using tools like az sql or specific drivers and run user creation scripts.

Common Error Resolution

Error: Invalid parameter group
Cause: Engine version incompatible with the parameter group.
Solution: Use the correct parameter group (e.g., default.postgres14 for PostgreSQL 14).

Error: Insufficient storage
Cause: The configured storage size does not meet the provider's minimum requirements.
Solution: Increase the allocated_storage or storage_mb parameter.

Error: Connection refused
Cause: Missing security group, firewall, or network configuration.

Solution: Ensure the database is accessible from the authorized client and that the ports are open.

Error: Invalid credentials
Cause: Incorrect username or password.
Solution: Check the variables passed in Terraform and avoid hardcoding.

Error: User already exists
Cause: Attempting to recreate an existing user.
Solution: Use terraform import to bring the user into the state or adjust the configuration.

Best Practices

- Never hardcode passwords in Terraform code; use terraform.tfvars or secret vaults.

- Configure automatic backups with periods aligned to the business's RTO/RPO.

- Use sensitive outputs (sensitive = true) to avoid exposing passwords and connection strings.

- Separate databases by environment (dev, stage, prod) using workspaces or .tfvars files.

- Configure logs and metrics to monitor performance and usage.

- Use modules to standardize deployment across providers.

- Enable data encryption at rest and in transit.

- Run backup restore tests periodically.

- Ensure network isolation for critical databases.

- Document users, permissions, and the purpose of each database.

Strategic Summary

Provisioning databases with Terraform transforms the deployment and data management process into something predictable, auditable, and replicable. PostgreSQL and MySQL can be delivered with consistent configurations, while backups ensure operational resilience. Careful management of users and permissions is fundamental to maintaining data security and integrity.

The most common errors, when well understood, become opportunities for learning and technical maturity. The disciplined use of the best practices described ensures not only a functional environment but also a secure operation aligned with business objectives.

CHAPTER 14. KUBERNETES CLUSTER DEPLOYMENT

Deploying Kubernetes clusters with Terraform is one of the most important steps for teams seeking advanced container orchestration in productive, scalable, and secure environments. Using Terraform, it's possible to provision clusters on providers like AWS (EKS), Google Cloud (GKE), and Azure (AKS), automate essential configurations, integrate tools like Helm to manage Kubernetes packages, and apply best practices for security and governance. This chapter explores each of these topics in depth, presenting practical examples, detailing common errors and their solutions, listing best practices, and concluding with a strategic summary that ties the entire operation to the organizational context.

Cluster Provisioning

Terraform allows the creation of Kubernetes clusters on major cloud providers using specific resources. Provisioning involves configuring virtual machines, networks, storage, authentication, and, in some cases, installing basic cluster components.

AWS EKS (Elastic Kubernetes Service)

Provisioning EKS involves three main resources: cluster, node group, and IAM role.

hcl

```
resource "aws_eks_cluster" "eks_cluster" {
  name    = "eks-cluster"
```

```
  role_arn = aws_iam_role.eks_role.arn


  vpc_config {
    subnet_ids = [aws_subnet.subnet1.id,
aws_subnet.subnet2.id]
  }
}


resource "aws_eks_node_group" "eks_nodes" {
  cluster_name    = aws_eks_cluster.eks_cluster.name
  node_group_name = "eks-nodes"
  node_role_arn   = aws_iam_role.eks_node_role.arn
  subnet_ids      = [aws_subnet.subnet1.id,
aws_subnet.subnet2.id]


  scaling_config {
    desired_size = 2
    max_size     = 3
    min_size     = 1
  }


  instance_types = ["t3.medium"]
}
```

Additionally, you need to create IAM roles and policies that allow

EKS to manage the resources.

Google Kubernetes Engine (GKE)

On GKE, deployment is more straightforward, as Google manages many details automatically.

hcl

```hcl
resource "google_container_cluster" "gke_cluster" {
  name     = "gke-cluster"
  location = "us-central1"


  initial_node_count = 3


  node_config {
    machine_type = "e2-medium"
  }
}
```

Azure Kubernetes Service (AKS)

On AKS, the azurerm_kubernetes_cluster resource creates the cluster and defines the agent node configuration.

hcl

```hcl
resource "azurerm_kubernetes_cluster" "aks_cluster" {
  name                = "aks-cluster"
  location            = azurerm_resource_group.rg.location
  resource_group_name = azurerm_resource_group.rg.name
  dns_prefix          = "akscluster"
```

```
default_node_pool {
  name      = "default"
  node_count = 2
  vm_size   = "Standard_DS2_v2"
}


identity {
  type = "SystemAssigned"
}
}
```

Automated Configuration

Once the cluster is provisioned, the next step is to automatically configure the components that enable the application to function correctly. This includes generating the kubeconfig file, configuring namespaces, applying RBAC policies, defining ingress controllers, and connecting storage.

Generate kubeconfig

Terraform can generate the kubeconfig using local_file or external commands.

hcl

```
data "aws_eks_cluster" "eks" {
  name = aws_eks_cluster.eks_cluster.name
}
```

```hcl
data "aws_eks_cluster_auth" "eks" {
  name = aws_eks_cluster.eks_cluster.name
}
```

```hcl
provider "kubernetes" {
  host            = data.aws_eks_cluster.eks.endpoint
  cluster_ca_certificate =
base64decode(data.aws_eks_cluster.eks.certificate_authority[0]
.data)
  token           = data.aws_eks_cluster_auth.eks.token
}
```

Namespaces and RBAC

hcl

```hcl
resource "kubernetes_namespace" "dev" {
  metadata {
    name = "development"
  }
}
```

```hcl
resource "kubernetes_role" "dev_role" {
  metadata {
    name     = "dev-role"
    namespace = kubernetes_namespace.dev.metadata[0].name
```

```
  }

  rule {
    api_groups = [""]
    resources  = ["pods"]
    verbs      = ["get", "list", "watch"]
  }
}
```

These blocks automate the logical separation and permissions within the cluster.

Ingress Controller

We can provision ingress controllers using Helm charts integrated into Terraform.

Helm Integration

Helm is Kubernetes's package manager, allowing the installation of complex applications like NGINX, Prometheus, Grafana, or databases in just a few commands. Terraform integrates with Helm through the helm provider.

Example of installing ingress-nginx with Terraform and Helm:

hcl

```
provider "helm" {
  kubernetes {
    config_path = "~/.kube/config"
  }
}
```

```
resource "helm_release" "nginx_ingress" {
  name       = "nginx-ingress"
  repository = "https://kubernetes.github.io/ingress-nginx"
  chart      = "ingress-nginx"
  namespace  = "kube-system"
  version    = "4.0.6"
}
```

We can also manage advanced configurations by passing custom values:

h

```
resource "helm_release" "prometheus" {
  name       = "prometheus"
  repository = "https://prometheus-community.github.io/helm-charts"
  chart      = "prometheus"
  namespace  = "monitoring"

  values = [
    file("prometheus-values.yaml")
  ]
}
```

Common Error Resolution

Error: Cluster authentication failed
Cause: kubeconfig was not generated correctly or credentials expired.
Solution: Regenerate the kubeconfig using the provider CLI or the Terraform blocks aws_eks_cluster_auth, google_container_cluster, or azurerm_kubernetes_cluster.

Error: Insufficient node capacity
Cause: The number or size of nodes does not support the scheduled pods.
Solution: Increase the node pool size or distribute pods across more nodes.

Error: Helm chart installation timeout
Cause: Cluster is not ready or there are unresolved dependencies.
Solution: Validate that the cluster is operating correctly (kubectl get nodes) and check the chart's dependency configurations.

Error: Pod scheduling failure
Cause: Lack of resources, affinity restrictions, or taints.
Solution: Review the resources requested in the manifest, adjust tolerations and affinities.

Error: Kubernetes provider not configured
Cause: The kubernetes or helm provider cannot connect to the cluster.
Solution: Ensure that the kubeconfig is correct and properly referenced in Terraform.

Best Practices

- Use Terraform modules to isolate clusters, node pools, and Helm configurations.

- Enable native provider logs and metrics for monitoring (CloudWatch, Stackdriver, Azure Monitor).

- Configure namespaces to separate workloads by environment or team.

- Adopt RBAC based on the principle of least privilege.

- Use ingress controllers and TLS certificates for secure traffic.

- Enable automatic scaling with HPA (Horizontal Pod Autoscaler).

- Configure regular backups of persistent volumes.

- Document chart and cluster versions for traceability.

- Validate Kubernetes manifests with kubectl apply --dry-run before deployment.

- Automate readiness tests post-provisioning with scripts or CI/CD tools.

Strategic Summary

Deploying Kubernetes clusters with Terraform marks a milestone in the maturity of DevOps practices, consolidating infrastructure automation and application orchestration into a single workflow. By provisioning clusters on providers like AWS, Google Cloud, and Azure, teams ensure consistency, scalability, and robustness in their environments.

Automatic configuration transforms "empty" clusters into production-ready environments, with namespaces, RBAC, ingress controllers, and storage properly organized. Helm integration amplifies this power, allowing complex applications like monitoring services, databases, and traffic controllers to be managed in a standardized way.

Common day-to-day errors, when well understood, become learning shortcuts rather than bottlenecks. They highlight the importance of deeply understanding how Terraform, Kubernetes, and cloud integrations work.

CHAPTER 15. AIRFLOW PIPELINE DEPLOYMENT

Apache Airflow has become an essential tool for workflow orchestration and data pipelines in modern engineering environments. By integrating Terraform into the Airflow deployment, it's possible to automate not only the creation of the necessary infrastructure but also the initial configuration, DAG deployment, and activation of integrated monitoring, ensuring that pipelines run with resilience, predictability, and governance. This chapter explores the complete deployment of Airflow, DAG configuration, monitoring practices, common errors encountered by teams, and the best practices that help transform operations into a stable and scalable model. We conclude with a strategic summary that connects everything to the business and operational landscape.

Airflow Deployment

Airflow can be provisioned across various architectures: on virtual machines (VMs), Kubernetes containers, or managed services like Amazon MWAA, Google Cloud Composer, or Azure Data Factory with Airflow.

Deployment on EC2 + PostgreSQL (AWS)

In scenarios using virtual machines, we provision Airflow on EC2 instances and a PostgreSQL database for the backend.

hcl

```
resource "aws_instance" "airflow" {
  ami     = "ami-0c55b159cbfafe1f0"
```

```
  instance_type = "t3.medium"
  key_name    = "airflow-key"


  tags = {
   Name = "AirflowInstance"
  }
}


resource "aws_db_instance" "airflow_db" {
  identifier    = "airflowdb"
  engine       = "postgres"
  instance_class  = "db.t3.micro"
  allocated_storage = 20
  name       = "airflow"
  username     = "airflow_user"
  password     = var.db_password
  parameter_group_name = "default.postgres14"
  skip_final_snapshot = true
}
```

After deploying the machines, it's necessary to configure Airflow to point to the database and start the components (webserver, scheduler, and workers).

Deployment on Kubernetes (with Helm)

Using Kubernetes is a more modern and scalable approach, especially with integration via Helm charts.

hcl

```hcl
resource "helm_release" "airflow" {
  name       = "airflow"
  repository = "https://airflow.apache.org"
  chart      = "airflow"
  namespace  = "airflow"

  values = [
    file("airflow-values.yaml")
  ]
}
```

The airflow-values.yaml file should include configurations such as executor (CeleryExecutor or KubernetesExecutor), database connections, fernet_key, credentials, and scalability.

Deployment on Managed Services

On AWS, Amazon Managed Workflows for Apache Airflow (MWAA) enables deployment with Terraform:

hcl

```hcl
resource "aws_mwaa_environment" "airflow_env" {
  name              = "airflow-env"
  airflow_version   = "2.4.3"
  environment_class = "mw1.medium"
  execution_role_arn = aws_iam_role.mwaa_role.arn
  source_bucket_arn = aws_s3_bucket.dags_bucket.arn
}
```

Google Cloud Composer and Azure Data Factory also have equivalent blocks for creating managed environments.

DAG Configuration

DAGs (Directed Acyclic Graphs) represent the pipelines in Airflow. To configure them correctly:

- Create a local dags folder.

- Develop the DAGs in Python.

- Upload them to the storage backend used by Airflow.

Deployment on EC2

Mount a shared volume or use rsync/SSH to transfer the DAGs to the instance.

Deployment on Kubernetes

Configure the Helm chart to map a volume or bucket containing the DAGs:

yaml

```
dags:
  gitSync:
    enabled: true
    repo: "https://github.com/usuario/repo-airflow-dags"
    branch: "main"
```

Deployment on MWAA

Upload the DAGs to the S3 bucket pointed to by the MWAA environment:

bash

```
aws s3 cp my_dag.py s3://my-mwaa-bucket/dags/
```

Integrated Monitoring

Monitoring Airflow is critical to ensure pipelines function correctly. This involves:

- Enabling persistent logs.

- Integrating with observability tools (Prometheus, Grafana).

- Setting up alerts.

EC2/Kubernetes

Configure Airflow to send logs to a centralized solution like CloudWatch, Stackdriver, or Azure Monitor. In airflow.cfg:

ini

```
[logging]
remote_logging = True
remote_base_log_folder = s3://my-airflow-logs-bucket
remote_log_conn_id = s3_default
```

Helm + Prometheus

In the Helm chart, enable Prometheus metrics:

yaml

```
metrics:
  enabled: true
```

```
serviceMonitor:
  enabled: true
```

This allows Prometheus to collect metrics automatically.

MWAA and Cloud Composer

The managed services already integrate logs with native platforms and allow alert configuration through their dashboards.

Common Error Resolution

Error: Connection failed to metadata database
Cause: Incorrect database configuration in Airflow.
Solution: Review the sql_alchemy_conn and fernet_key variables; ensure the database is accessible.

Error: DAG not loaded
Cause: Parsing failure or DAG Python structure issue.
Solution: Run the command airflow dags list and check logs to identify syntax errors.

Error: Scheduler not running
Cause: Scheduler not started or stuck.
Solution: Check the scheduler logs and restart the process.

Error: Out of memory
Cause: Insufficient resources on the node or pod.
Solution: Increase the instance size or pod request/limit in Kubernetes.

Error: Helm chart upgrade failure
Cause: Version conflict or incompatible changes.
Solution: Run helm diff upgrade before applying or use --force.

Best Practices

- Use official or community-validated Helm charts.

- Enable RBAC and separate namespaces to isolate environments.

- Configure connections and variables in Airflow using Secrets.

- Use version control for DAGs (Git, CI/CD).

- Enable smart sensors to reduce scheduler load.

- Configure pools to limit task concurrency.

- Enable autoscaling in Kubernetes to adjust to load.

- Monitor DAG execution time and identify bottlenecks.

- Set SLAs in DAGs to trigger alerts.

- Periodically review DAGs and external dependencies.

Strategic Summary

Deploying Airflow pipelines with Terraform radically transforms how data teams orchestrate complex workflows, integrating data across systems and ensuring end-to-end traceability. Automating Airflow provisioning, along with DAG configuration and integrated monitoring, provides not only efficiency but also operational resilience.

Integration with Kubernetes and Helm extends technical reach, allowing pipelines to scale as business demands grow. Managed services like MWAA and Cloud Composer offer robust solutions for companies looking to reduce operational overhead without losing pipeline control.

CHAPTER 16. DEPLOYING MLFLOW FOR MLOPS

MLflow has become one of the central tools in the MLOps ecosystem, allowing teams to track experiments, manage models, store artifacts, and promote machine learning models to production in an organized and auditable way. When integrated with Terraform, deploying MLflow and its associated infrastructure gains an additional level of predictability and scalability. This chapter covers provisioning MLflow using Terraform, integrating it with pipelines, managing models, resolving common errors, and applying best practices that consolidate robust MLOps operations. We conclude with a strategic summary that connects these points to modern business and operational contexts.

Provisioning MLflow

MLflow can be deployed in multiple environments: local, on virtual machines, in Kubernetes, or integrated with managed services. Terraform allows you to provision the entire infrastructure base needed to host MLflow, including servers, storage, and backend databases.

Deploy on EC2 + PostgreSQL (AWS)

hcl

```
resource "aws_instance" "mlflow_server" {
  ami           = "ami-0c55b159cbfafe1f0"
  instance_type = "t3.medium"
```

```
  key_name    = "mlflow-key"

  tags = {
    Name = "MLflowServer"
  }
}


resource "aws_db_instance" "mlflow_db" {
  identifier      = "mlflowdb"
  engine          = "postgres"
  instance_class   = "db.t3.micro"
  allocated_storage = 20
  name          = "mlflow"
  username        = "mlflow_user"
  password        = var.db_password
  parameter_group_name = "default.postgres14"
  skip_final_snapshot = true
}
```

After provisioning the machines, install the MLflow Server pointing to the backend and storage:

bash

```
mlflow server \
    --backend-store-uri postgresql://
mlflow_user:password@mlflow-db-endpoint:5432/mlflow \
```

--default-artifact-root s3://mlflow-artifacts \

--host 0.0.0.0 --port 5000

Deploy on Kubernetes with Helm

On Kubernetes, MLflow deployment is more robust, and Helm simplifies the installation.

hcl

```hcl
resource "helm_release" "mlflow" {
  name      = "mlflow"
  repository = "https://community-charts.github.io/helm-charts"
  chart     = "mlflow"
  namespace = "mlops"


  values = [
    file("mlflow-values.yaml")
  ]
}
```

In the mlflow-values.yaml file, define the database endpoints, storage, and specific configurations, including environment variables and CPU/memory resources.

Integration with Pipelines

Integrating MLflow with machine learning pipelines allows you to track experiments, store metrics, and promote models automatically. The main steps of this integration are:

- Configure the backend tracking URI in the pipelines.

- Use MLflow APIs to log metrics, parameters, and artifacts.

- Automate the deployment of approved models.

Tracking URI Configuration

Inside the pipeline code (example in Python):

python

```python
import mlflow


mlflow.set_tracking_uri("http://mlflow-server:5000")
mlflow.set_experiment("my_experiment")


with mlflow.start_run():
    mlflow.log_param("param1", 10)
    mlflow.log_metric("metric1", 0.85)
    mlflow.sklearn.log_model(model, "model")
```

Automation with CI/CD

Use tools like GitHub Actions, GitLab CI, or Jenkins to trigger experiments, train models, and automatically register results. Example in GitHub Actions:

yaml

```yaml
- name: Run MLflow pipeline
  run: |
    mlflow run . -P alpha=0.5 -P l1_ratio=0.1
```

Model Management

MLflow offers robust features to manage models, including registration, versioning, and deployment. The Model Registry component facilitates model lifecycle control.

Register Model

python

```
import mlflow

result = mlflow.register_model(
    "runs:/<run_id>/model",
    "my_model"
)
```

Promote Model

python

```
from mlflow.tracking import MlflowClient

client = MlflowClient()
client.transition_model_version_stage(
    name="my_model",
    version=1,
    stage="Production"
)
```

Serve Model

Run a model as a REST API:

bash

```
mlflow models serve -m models:/my_model/Production -p 1234
```

This approach makes it easy to create APIs that can be integrated directly into production applications.

Common Error Resolution

Error: Database connection failed
Cause: Incorrect backend configuration or unavailable database.
Solution: Check the connection string, ensure the database port is open, and verify credentials.

Error: S3 bucket permission denied
Cause: Missing permissions on the S3 bucket to store artifacts.
Solution: Ensure the role or user has s3:PutObject and s3:GetObject policies.

Error: Incompatible MLflow client/server version
Cause: Version mismatch between MLflow client and server.
Solution: Align the versions installed in the local environment and server.

Error: Model stage transition error
Cause: Lack of permissions in the Model Registry.
Solution: Configure users and permissions correctly on the MLflow Tracking Server.

Error: Helm chart deploy failed
Cause: Resource conflict or incompatible configurations.
Solution: Validate the values.yaml file, use helm lint and helm diff upgrade before applying.

Best Practices

- Use Terraform to automate not only deployment but also MLflow infrastructure versioning.

- Separate environments (dev, stage, prod) using workspaces and .tfvars files.

- Configure TLS for secure access to the MLflow Server.

- Integrate MLflow with authentication sources (OAuth2, LDAP) for access control.

- Version experiments and pipelines in Git.

- Use tags on experiments to facilitate search and filtering.

- Periodically clean up old runs and artifacts to reduce storage costs.

- Configure monitoring (Prometheus, Grafana) for the MLflow infrastructure.

- Automate deployment of approved models with CI/CD pipelines.

- Clearly document the model lifecycle in the Model Registry.

Strategic Summary

Deploying MLflow using Terraform consolidates the pillars of traceability and governance in MLOps operations, ensuring that experiments, models, and metrics are treated as business assets. By provisioning infrastructure declaratively and connecting it directly to automated pipelines, teams gain agility, reproducibility, and confidence across the entire machine learning lifecycle.

Integration with pipelines elevates operational maturity, enabling the monitoring of experiments at scale, comparing results, and automating deployments to production. Careful model management with the Model Registry ensures that only approved versions are available for use in critical environments.

CHAPTER 17. AUTOMATION WITH CI/CD (GITHUB ACTIONS, GITLAB CI)

Automation with CI/CD (Continuous Integration and Continuous Delivery) pipelines is a game changer for teams working with Terraform, enabling infrastructure, applications, and tests to be orchestrated in a predictable, scalable, and auditable manner. Platforms like GitHub Actions and GitLab CI have become essential in this process, making it possible to automatically validate, apply, and monitor infrastructure changes with Terraform. This chapter explores how to set up Terraform pipelines using these platforms, integrate automated tests, enable continuous deployment, address common errors, and apply best practices that ensure efficiency and security. We finish with a strategic summary that ties the technical impact to organizational value.

Terraform Pipeline

In a CI/CD context, a well-designed Terraform pipeline ensures that every infrastructure code change goes through validation and approval before being applied to the production environment. The fundamental steps of a pipeline are:

- Initialization (terraform init)

- Validation (terraform validate)

- Formatting (terraform fmt)

- **Planning** (terraform plan)

- **Application** (terraform apply)

- **(Optional) Destruction** (terraform destroy **in temporary environments)**

Example with GitHub Actions

yaml

```
name: Terraform Pipeline

on:
  push:
    branches:
      - main

jobs:
  terraform:
    runs-on: ubuntu-latest

    steps:
    - name: Checkout code
      uses: actions/checkout@v2

    - name: Setup Terraform
      uses: hashicorp/setup-terraform@v2
```

```yaml
- name: Terraform Init
  run: terraform init

- name: Terraform Format
  run: terraform fmt -check

- name: Terraform Validate
  run: terraform validate

- name: Terraform Plan
  run: terraform plan

- name: Terraform Apply
  if: github.ref == 'refs/heads/main'
  run: terraform apply -auto-approve
```

Example with GitLab CI

yaml

```yaml
stages:
  - init
  - validate
  - plan
  - apply
```

```
variables:
  TF_ROOT: .

init:
  stage: init
  script:
    - terraform init

validate:
  stage: validate
  script:
    - terraform validate

plan:
  stage: plan
  script:
    - terraform plan -out=tfplan

apply:
  stage: apply
  when: manual
  script:
    - terraform apply -auto-approve tfplan
```

These examples ensure that the code is validated and applied in an orderly and transparent manner, building trust in the changes.

Test Automation

Test automation in CI/CD pipelines for Terraform mainly involves:

- **Static tests:** terraform validate, terraform fmt

- **Security tests:** integration with tools like Checkov, tfsec, or Terrascan

- **Unit tests and mocks:** using frameworks such as Terratest or kitchen-terraform

Example with Checkov in GitHub Actions

yaml
```
- name: Run Checkov scan
  uses: bridgecrewio/checkov-action@master
  with:
    directory: .
```

Example with tfsec in GitLab CI

yaml
```
tfsec:
  stage: validate
  script:
    - curl -s https://raw.githubusercontent.com/aquasecurity/
```

```
tfsec/master/scripts/install_linux.sh | bash

  - tfsec .
```

These tools scan Terraform code for bad practices, vulnerabilities, and non-compliance before it reaches production.

Continuous Deployment

Continuous deployment with Terraform means that approved changes in the repository are automatically applied to the target environment without manual intervention. To achieve this, it is recommended to:

- Manage the state in a remote backend (S3, Google Cloud Storage, Azure Storage)

- Use workspaces to separate environments (dev, staging, prod)

- Protect branches with approval rules

- Configure pipelines with manual stages for sensitive environments

Example of environment control in GitHub Actions

yaml

```
- name: Terraform Apply Dev
  if: github.ref == 'refs/heads/dev'
  run: terraform apply -auto-approve


- name: Terraform Apply Prod
  if: github.ref == 'refs/heads/main'
```

run: terraform apply -auto-approve

Remote backend configuration in Terraform

hcl

```
terraform {
  backend "s3" {
    bucket = "my-tfstate"
    key   = "infra/terraform.tfstate"
    region = "us-east-1"
  }
}
```

This ensures that multiple pipelines and users can work simultaneously without overwriting the state.

Common Error Resolution

Error: Error acquiring the state lock
Cause: Two pipelines or manual executions trying to access the same state concurrently.
Solution: Configure remote locking in the backend, review parallelism, and if necessary, manually unlock using force-unlock commands.

Error: Provider plugin not found
Cause: Different Terraform versions or missing provider in the pipeline environment.
Solution: Use hashicorp/setup-terraform to ensure the correct version or explicitly configure providers in the code.

Error: Secrets or credentials missing

Cause: Missing environment variables in CI/CD.
Solution: Configure secrets in GitHub (Settings → Secrets) or GitLab (CI/CD → Variables) and reference them correctly.

Error: Failed plan due to drift
Cause: Differences between the current state and the code.
Solution: Run terraform refresh or terraform plan to identify unmanaged changes.

Error: Manual approval missing in sensitive stage
Cause: Continuous deployment without a manual gate in a critical environment.
Solution: Configure when: manual in GitLab or required reviewers in GitHub for production stages.

Best Practices

- Use dedicated branches for each environment and protect main and prod with required reviews.

- Store the state in remote backends with locking enabled.

- Separate pipelines by environment using workspaces or directories.

- Integrate security and compliance checks automatically.

- Document pipelines, variables, and secrets in the repository.

- Keep pipelines fast and lean, parallelizing steps when possible.

- Audit execution logs and configure failure alerts.

- Test pipelines in isolated environments before promoting to production.

- Regularly update pipeline tools (Terraform, Checkov, tfsec).

- Train the team to interpret failures and adjust configurations quickly.

Strategic Summary

Automation with CI/CD transforms how organizations handle infrastructure and applications, enabling rapid, secure, and auditable changes. With GitHub Actions and GitLab CI, Terraform pipelines become not just scripts but true infrastructure orchestrators, ensuring that every change goes through testing, validation, and deployment transparently.

Test automation increases confidence, reduces human error, and anticipates vulnerabilities that could compromise operations. Continuous deployment, in turn, frees teams to focus on innovation instead of repetitive tasks, maintaining alignment between development and operations.

CHAPTER 18. SECURITY AND COMPLIANCE

Security and compliance are fundamental pillars in managing infrastructure as code with Terraform, especially in corporate environments handling sensitive data, regulations, and audits. Ignoring these concerns can lead to serious breaches, financial losses, and reputational damage. This chapter presents in detail how to implement policies and roles, apply validation and linting, protect sensitive data, resolve common errors, and adopt best practices. It concludes with a strategic summary connecting these aspects to a mature, secure, and business-aligned operation.

Policies and Roles

Controlling who can do what in the infrastructure is essential to minimizing risk. Terraform integrates with cloud providers and external tools to manage policies and roles, ensuring that only authorized users or processes can perform specific actions.

AWS IAM Policies and Roles

hcl

```
resource "aws_iam_role" "terraform_role" {
  name = "terraform-role"

  assume_role_policy = jsonencode({
    Version = "2012-10-17",
```

```
    Statement = [{
      Effect   = "Allow",
      Principal = {
        Service = "ec2.amazonaws.com"
      },
      Action   = "sts:AssumeRole"
    }]
  })
}


resource "aws_iam_policy" "terraform_policy" {
  name       = "terraform-policy"
  description = "Policy for Terraform"

  policy = jsonencode({
    Version = "2012-10-17",
    Statement = [{
      Effect   = "Allow",
      Action   = ["ec2:*", "s3:*"],
      Resource = "*"
    }]
  })
}


resource "aws_iam_role_policy_attachment" "attach" {
```

```hcl
  role       = aws_iam_role.terraform_role.name
  policy_arn = aws_iam_policy.terraform_policy.arn
}
```

Google Cloud IAM

hcl

```hcl
resource "google_project_iam_member" "terraform_member" {
  project = var.project_id
  role    = "roles/editor"
  member  = "serviceAccount:terraform@my-project.iam.gserviceaccount.com"
}
```

Azure Role Assignment

hcl

```hcl
resource "azurerm_role_assignment" "terraform_assignment" {
  principal_id        = azurerm_user_assigned_identity.identity.principal_id
  role_definition_name = "Contributor"
  scope               = azurerm_resource_group.rg.id
}
```

These configurations prevent excessive permissions and help apply the principle of least privilege.

Validation and Linting

Validation and linting help identify security issues, style

problems, and best practice violations before deployment, reducing risk and improving code quality.

Terraform Validate

Performs syntax and logic checks.

bash

```
terraform validate
```

Terraform Fmt

Ensures consistent formatting.

bash

```
terraform fmt -check
```

Checkov

Security tool that detects insecure configurations.

bash

```
checkov -d .
```

tfsec

Scanner that highlights known vulnerabilities.

bash

```
tfsec .
```

TFLint

Linter to detect syntax errors and discouraged practices.

bash

```
tflint
```

Integrating these tools into the CI/CD pipeline makes the process continuous and standardized.

Protection of Sensitive Data

Keeping sensitive data secure is a critical requirement. Passwords, tokens, and API keys should never be hardcoded in Terraform code or repositories.

Sensitive Variables

```hcl
variable "db_password" {
  type     = string
  sensitive = true
}
```

Passing Variables via CLI

```bash
terraform apply -var "db_password=${DB_PASSWORD}"
```

Using Secure Backends

Configure S3 with encryption, Google Cloud Storage, or Azure Storage with versioning and access protection.

```hcl
terraform {
  backend "s3" {
    bucket     = "my-secure-bucket"
```

```
key         = "terraform.tfstate"
region      = "us-east-1"
encrypt     = true
dynamodb_table = "terraform-lock"
}
}
```

Secrets Vaults

Integrate Terraform with HashiCorp Vault, AWS Secrets Manager, Google Secret Manager, or Azure Key Vault to dynamically access secrets.

hcl

```
data "vault_generic_secret" "db_password" {
  path = "secret/data/db_password"
}
```

Common Error Resolution

Error: Insufficient permissions
Cause: Incomplete role or policy.
Solution: Review permissions, apply the principle of least privilege, and only add necessary actions.

Error: Unencrypted state file
Cause: Misconfigured backend.
Solution: Enable backend encryption, use locks, and restrict bucket access.

Error: Secret in plain text
Cause: Secret exposed in code.
Solution: Replace with a sensitive variable, remove from Git

history, and store in a secrets vault.

Error: Policy too permissive
Cause: Use of wildcard (*) in actions or resources.
Solution: Refine policies to cover only required resources and actions.

Error: Compliance check failed
Cause: Failure in tools like Checkov or tfsec.
Solution: Correct the tool recommendations before proceeding with deployment.

Best Practices

- Apply the principle of least privilege across all resources.

- Use automatic linting and validation tools on every commit.

- Manage the state in secure, encrypted backends.

- Integrate secrets vaults to store and retrieve sensitive data.

- Configure alerts and logs to monitor policy and role changes.

- Periodically audit permissions and remove unnecessary access.

- Separate environments (dev, stage, prod) using workspaces.

- Clearly document policies and security architecture.

- Conduct code reviews for changes to critical resources.

- Train the team on handling secrets, permissions, and

compliance.

Strategic Summary

Security and compliance in Terraform projects go far beyond avoiding technical failures: they ensure that IT operations align with legal requirements, business expectations, and global best practices. Implementing correct policies and roles reduces the attack surface and protects the most valuable resources. Applying validation and linting ensures that the code is clean, consistent, and aligned with standards. Protecting sensitive data is both an ethical and regulatory obligation, mitigating risks that could compromise organizational trust.

Understanding and solving common errors demonstrates technical maturity and operational resilience. The best practices described in this chapter not only raise security levels but also make processes more efficient, auditable, and robust.

CHAPTER 19. MONITORING WITH PROMETHEUS AND GRAFANA

Monitoring with Prometheus and Grafana has become essential in modern infrastructure environments, especially when operating with Terraform, Kubernetes, cloud, and distributed applications. These tools allow you to visualize metrics, identify anomalies, detect bottlenecks, and proactively respond to incidents. When integrated into the Terraform cycle, Prometheus and Grafana provide complete visibility over infrastructure, pipelines, and services, promoting more resilient and predictable operations. This chapter explores how to configure Terraform exporters, build efficient dashboards, enable automated alerts, handle common errors, and implement best practices to establish a robust and reliable monitoring environment. We conclude with a strategic summary that connects these elements to organizational impact.

Terraform Exporters

To collect metrics from environments provisioned with Terraform, we use exporters — components that expose metrics in a format understood by Prometheus. While Terraform itself does not have a native exporter, the provisioned infrastructure can be instrumented with specific exporters depending on the context.

Node Exporter (Provisioned Machines)

On virtual machines created with Terraform (AWS EC2, Google

Compute Engine, Azure VMs), install Node Exporter:

hcl

```
resource "null_resource" "install_node_exporter" {
  provisioner "remote-exec" {
    inline = [
      "wget https://github.com/prometheus/node_exporter/releases/download/v1.3.1/node_exporter-1.3.1.linux-amd64.tar.gz",
      "tar xvfz node_exporter-1.3.1.linux-amd64.tar.gz",
      "sudo mv node_exporter-1.3.1.linux-amd64/node_exporter /usr/local/bin/",
      "sudo useradd -rs /bin/false node_exporter",
      "sudo tee /etc/systemd/system/node_exporter.service <<EOF",
      "[Unit]",
      "Description=Node Exporter",
      "[Service]",
      "User=node_exporter",
      "ExecStart=/usr/local/bin/node_exporter",
      "[Install]",
      "WantedBy=default.target",
      "EOF",
      "sudo systemctl daemon-reload",
      "sudo systemctl start node_exporter",
      "sudo systemctl enable node_exporter"
    ]
```

```
connection {
  type      = "ssh"
  user      = "ec2-user"
  private_key = file("~/.ssh/id_rsa")
  host      = aws_instance.meu_servidor.public_ip
  }
 }
}
```

Kube State Metrics (Kubernetes)

In Kubernetes clusters created with Terraform, include kube-state-metrics to monitor cluster resources:

hcl

```
resource "helm_release" "kube_state_metrics" {
  name     = "kube-state-metrics"
  repository = "https://prometheus-community.github.io/helm-charts"
  chart    = "kube-state-metrics"
  namespace = "monitoring"
}
```

Cloud Exporters

- AWS → CloudWatch Exporter
- Google Cloud → Stackdriver Exporter
- Azure → Azure Monitor Exporter

Each requires specific permissions configured with Terraform and exposing metrics on endpoints visible to Prometheus.

Dashboards

With metrics being collected, configure dashboards in Grafana to turn data into insights.

Provisioning Grafana with Terraform

hcl

```hcl
resource "grafana_dashboard" "node_dashboard" {
  config_json = file("node_exporter_dashboard.json")
}
```

This JSON can be exported directly from the Grafana UI after manual setup or generated with tools like grafonnet and grizzly.

Recommended Dashboards

- Infrastructure (CPU, RAM, disk, network per host)

- Kubernetes (pods, nodes, deployments, namespaces)

- Databases (PostgreSQL, MySQL, MongoDB)

- Applications (latency, throughput, errors, queues)

- CI/CD pipeline (build time, failures, success by branch)

Well-designed dashboards avoid excessive graphs, organize metrics by context (infrastructure, application, network), and facilitate quick visual reading.

Automated Alerts

Automated alerts allow you to act before incidents become

critical. Prometheus and Grafana offer native alerting mechanisms.

Alerting with Prometheus

yaml

```
groups:
- name: node_alerts
  rules:
  - alert: HighCPUUsage
    expr: 100 - (avg by(instance)
(irate(node_cpu_seconds_total{mode="idle"}[5m])) * 100) > 90
    for: 5m
    labels:
      severity: critical
    annotations:
      summary: "High CPU usage on {{ $labels.instance }}"
      description: "CPU usage is above 90% for 5 minutes."
```

Integrating with Alertmanager

yaml

```
receivers:
- name: slack-notifications
  slack_configs:
  - channel: "#alerts"
    send_resolved: true
```

Alerts in Grafana

Grafana allows you to create alerts directly on dashboards:

- Access the panel → Alert → Create alert → Define conditions and thresholds → Configure notifications for Slack, Email, or Webhooks.

Common Error Resolution

Error: Exporter not reachable
Cause: Missing network permissions or firewall blocking the port.
Solution: Open the port in the security group or configure VPC peering.

Error: High cardinality metrics
Cause: Metrics with too many unique labels, causing excessive memory use.
Solution: Filter out irrelevant labels in Prometheus scrape config.

Error: Alert flood
Cause: Too-sensitive alert conditions.
Solution: Adjust thresholds and for time to reduce false positives.

Error: Dashboard provisioning failed
Cause: Invalid or incompatible JSON.
Solution: Validate the JSON in Grafana before importing via Terraform.

Error: Disk full on Prometheus server
Cause: Poorly configured metric retention.
Solution: Reduce --storage.tsdb.retention.time and configure a larger volume.

Best Practices

- Use official exporters and keep them updated.

- Limit the scrape interval for less critical metrics.

- Separate Prometheus and Grafana in isolated namespaces and clusters.

- Document each dashboard and its purpose.

- Use alerts with differentiated severities (warning, critical).

- Store dashboard JSONs in Git for versioning.

- Regularly test alerts to avoid alert fatigue.

- Configure metric retention compatible with business objectives.

- Integrate cost metrics (AWS Billing, GCP Billing) to monitor expenses.

- Automate monitoring deployments using Terraform and CI/CD pipelines.

Strategic Summary

Monitoring with Prometheus and Grafana, integrated with Terraform, transforms reactive operations into proactive ones. By properly instrumenting infrastructure with exporters, configuring dashboards aligned with technical context, and enabling automated alerts, teams gain unprecedented visibility and response capabilities.

More than just collecting metrics, effective monitoring organizes data into understandable stories that guide decisions, detect failures, and optimize resources. Resolving common errors and adopting best practices ensures the monitoring environment is robust, efficient, and aligned with business needs.

CHAPTER 20. INTEGRATION WITH ANSIBLE

The integration between Terraform and Ansible is a powerful combination for modern infrastructure and configuration operations. Terraform provisions the base infrastructure — virtual machines, networks, storage, load balancers — while Ansible steps in to configure the operating system, install packages, manage services, and apply hardening. This clear separation of responsibilities provides flexibility, modularity, and scalability for DevOps and infrastructure teams. Below, we detail the mechanisms for cross-calling between Terraform and Ansible, the creation of automated playbooks, a practical example, common errors and solutions, best practices, and a strategic summary that connects operations to business value.

Cross-call Terraform → Ansible

The Terraform → Ansible flow works in three main steps:

- Terraform provisions infrastructure (EC2, GCE, Azure VM, etc.)

- Terraform generates dynamic inventory files or hosts files.

- Terraform triggers Ansible playbooks using local provisioners, local-exec modules, or CI/CD integrations.

Inventory Generation

Terraform can dynamically generate an inventory file to be used by Ansible:

h

```
resource "local_file" "inventory" {
  content = templatefile("${path.module}/inventory.tpl", {
    ip = aws_instance.servidor.public_ip
  })
  filename = "${path.module}/inventory.ini"
}
```

Example of inventory.tpl:

bash

```
[web]
${ip} ansible_user=ec2-user
```

Automatic Execution

With the inventory ready, Terraform can call Ansible:

hcl

```
resource "null_resource" "ansible_provision" {
  provisioner "local-exec" {
    command = "ANSIBLE_HOST_KEY_CHECKING=False
ansible-playbook -i ${local_file.inventory.filename}
playbook.yml"
  }
}
```

This model seamlessly connects both worlds, ensuring that configuration occurs right after provisioning.

Automated Playbooks

Ansible playbooks are YAML scripts that describe the desired configuration for provisioned machines. They can automate everything from package installation to application and service configuration.

Basic playbook example:

yaml

```
- name: Configure web servers
  hosts: web
  become: yes
  tasks:
    - name: Install Nginx
      apt:
        name: nginx
        state: present
        update_cache: yes

    - name: Enable and start Nginx
      systemd:
        name: nginx
        enabled: yes
        state: started
```

This playbook can be automatically referenced after Terraform deploy, ensuring each machine exits the pipeline already configured and ready for use. More advanced playbooks may include handlers, Jinja2 templates, roles, vaults for passwords, and tags for selective execution.

Practical Example

Provision an EC2 with Terraform and automatically configure it with Ansible.

1. Terraform Code

hcl

```
provider "aws" {
  region = "us-east-1"
}


resource "aws_instance" "web" {
    ami        = "ami-0c55b159cbfafe1f0"
    instance_type = "t3.micro"
    key_name    = "my-key"


  tags = {
    Name = "WebServer"
  }
}


resource "local_file" "inventory" {
  content = "[web]\n${aws_instance.web.public_ip}
ansible_user=ec2-user"
  filename = "${path.module}/inventory.ini"
}
```

```
resource "null_resource" "ansible" {
  depends_on = [aws_instance.web]


  provisioner "local-exec" {
    command = "ANSIBLE_HOST_KEY_CHECKING=False
ansible-playbook -i ${local_file.inventory.filename}
playbook.yml"
  }
}
```

2. Ansible Playbook (playbook.yml)

yaml

```
- name: Configure webserver
  hosts: web
  become: yes
  tasks:
    - name: Install Apache
      yum:
        name: httpd
        state: present

    - name: Start Apache
      service:
```

```
name: httpd

state: started

enabled: yes
```

Such a flow ensures that after Terraform spins up the instance, Ansible automatically configures Apache on the server.

Common Error Resolution

Error: SSH authentication failure
Cause: Missing or incorrect SSH key, wrong user.
Solution: Ensure the private key used by Ansible matches the one configured in Terraform and that the user is correct in the inventory.

Error: Host unreachable
Cause: Firewall blocking SSH port or machine not ready.
Solution: Check firewall rules, configure security groups in Terraform, and add a pause in the playbook if needed.

Error: Inventory file missing or malformed
Cause: Poorly generated dynamic inventory.
Solution: Validate the Terraform template, use terraform output to generate correct IPs, and test inventory with ansible-inventory --list.

Error: Local-exec command fails silently
Cause: Lack of detailed logs in Terraform.
Solution: Use set -eux in the called scripts to capture errors and print relevant outputs.

Error: Ansible variables not passed
Cause: Missing integration between Terraform outputs and Ansible vars.
Solution: Generate a .yml file with local_file and include it with -e @vars.yml in the playbook.

Best Practices

- Separate Terraform into modules and Ansible into roles for maximum reuse.

- Configure CI/CD pipelines to orchestrate Terraform and Ansible in an orderly fashion.

- Use tags in Ansible to execute only specific parts of the playbook during updates.

- Configure Vault or Ansible Vault to protect sensitive variables.

- Use Ansible Dynamic Inventory to integrate with cloud APIs in larger environments.

- Maintain idempotency in Ansible so running the playbook multiple times has no side effects.

- Document dependencies between Terraform and Ansible so the team understands the flow.

- Run terraform apply with -auto-approve only in controlled environments.

- Perform tests with ansible-playbook --check to validate playbooks before applying them.

Strategic Summary

The integration between Terraform and Ansible creates a complete cycle of provisioning and configuration, allowing teams to deliver infrastructure and applications already prepared for production quickly and safely. Terraform ensures that resources are available in a standardized and auditable way; Ansible transforms these resources into ready, consistent environments aligned with business requirements.

The smart use of cross-calls, automated playbooks, and orchestrated pipelines dramatically reduces the time between infrastructure creation and value delivery. Knowing and resolving common errors ensures process fluidity, while best practices strengthen governance and technical quality.

CHAPTER 21. INTEGRATION WITH JENKINS

Integrating Terraform with Jenkins is a powerful step to transform CI/CD pipelines into complete and reliable delivery flows, combining the robustness of one of the most popular orchestrators in the DevOps world with the flexibility of Terraform to manage infrastructure. This integration allows teams to manage not only the software lifecycle but also infrastructure as code, offering end-to-end automation, auditing, and traceability. This chapter explores how to build declarative pipelines in Jenkins, connect this automation with CI/CD flows, present a real example, resolve common errors, and apply best practices to strengthen operations and continuous delivery. We conclude with a strategic summary that highlights the impact of this integration for technical teams and the business.

Declarative Pipeline

In Jenkins, the declarative pipeline is the most popular and modern format for describing automation. It allows defining stages, conditions, environment, agents, and actions in an organized and standardized manner.

A basic Terraform pipeline includes:

- Environment preparation: repository checkout, Terraform installation.

- Validation: terraform fmt, terraform validate.

- Planning: terraform plan.

- Application: terraform apply.

Example of a declarative pipeline in Jenkinsfile:

groovy

```groovy
pipeline {
    agent any

    environment {
        TF_VERSION = '1.4.6'
    }

    stages {
        stage('Checkout') {
            steps {
                checkout scm
            }
        }

        stage('Install Terraform') {
            steps {
                sh 'wget https://releases.hashicorp.com/terraform/${TF_VERSION}/terraform_${TF_VERSION}_linux_amd64.zip'
                sh 'unzip terraform_${TF_VERSION}_linux_amd64.zip'
                sh 'sudo mv terraform /usr/local/bin/'
```

```
        }
    }

    stage('Init') {
        steps {
            sh 'terraform init'
        }
    }

    stage('Validate') {
        steps {
            sh 'terraform fmt -check'
            sh 'terraform validate'
        }
    }

    stage('Plan') {
        steps {
            sh 'terraform plan -out=tfplan'
        }
    }

    stage('Apply') {
        when {
            branch 'main'
```

```
    }
    steps {
        input message: 'Approve application?', ok: 'Approve'
        sh 'terraform apply -auto-approve tfplan'
    }
  }
}


post {
    always {
        archiveArtifacts          artifacts:          '**/*.tfplan',
allowEmptyArchive: true
    }
  }
}
```

This pipeline performs essential Terraform steps, requires manual approval for sensitive environments, and archives the plan for traceability.

CI/CD Integration

Complete CI/CD integration with Jenkins and Terraform goes beyond the simple pipeline: it connects code, infrastructure, and application in a single flow.

Essential components:

- Version control (GitHub, GitLab, Bitbucket): Jenkins should listen to commits, pull requests, or merges.

- Secrets management: use Jenkins Credentials to store tokens, SSH keys, and sensitive variables.

- Notifications: integrate Slack, email, or Microsoft Teams to alert about changes and failures.

- Multibranch pipeline: configure separate pipelines by branch (dev, staging, prod).

Example of triggers in Jenkinsfile:

groovy

```groovy
triggers {
    githubPush()
}
```

In Jenkins, configure the webhook in the repository to automatically notify on each push.

Example

Imagine a team needing to provision Kubernetes clusters on AWS, configure storage on S3, and apply security policies. The real flow would look like:

- Developer commits to the dev branch → Jenkins triggers the pipeline.

- Pipeline executes:

  - terraform fmt, validate, plan.

  - Creates EKS clusters and S3 buckets.

  - Updates IAM rules.

- Apply stage requires manual approval in Jenkins:

  - User approves.

  - terraform apply runs.

- Slack notification about success/failure.

Adapted Jenkinsfile:

groovy

```groovy
pipeline {
    agent any

    stages {
        stage('Checkout') {
            steps { checkout scm }
        }

        stage('Terraform Init') {
            steps { sh 'terraform init' }
        }

        stage('Terraform Plan') {
            steps { sh 'terraform plan -out=tfplan' }
        }
```

```
stage('Approval and Apply') {
    when { branch 'main' }
    steps {
        input message: 'Approve deploy?', ok: 'Approve'
        sh 'terraform apply -auto-approve tfplan'
    }
}
}


post {
    success {
        slackSend channel: '#deployments', message:
"Successful deployment on main environment."
    }
    failure {
        slackSend channel: '#alerts', message: "Deployment
error on main environment."
    }
}
}
```

Common Error Resolution

Error: Terraform binary not found
Cause: Terraform not installed on Jenkins agent.
Solution: Install Terraform in the container, machine, or use

hashicorp/setup-terraform in declarative pipelines.

Error: Credentials not provided
Cause: Missing secrets in Jenkins.
Solution: Configure Jenkins Credentials and inject them into the pipeline environment.

Error: Concurrent apply conflict
Cause: Parallel executions applying to the same backend.
Solution: Enable locking in the remote backend and serialize executions with queues in Jenkins.

Error: Plan differs from applied state
Cause: External changes in the environment (drift).
Solution: Run terraform refresh before plan to sync state.

Error: Approval stage bypassed
Cause: Pipeline missing manual stage in critical branch.
Solution: Configure mandatory input before apply.

Best Practices

- Separate pipelines by environment with multibranch or directories (dev, stage, prod).

- Use terraform plan as a mandatory gate before apply.

- Protect critical branches with pull requests and reviews.

- Configure manual rollback in case of deployment failure.

- Use Terraform modules to avoid code duplication.

- Store state in remote backends with locking enabled.

- Integrate security analysis (Checkov, tfsec) in the pipeline.

- Use parameterized pipelines to select environment and

variables.

- Document pipelines and approval flows in the repository.

- Periodically review Jenkins permissions and agents.

Strategic Summary

Integrating Jenkins with Terraform elevates infrastructure automation to a new level, transforming pipelines into consistent, auditable, and fast flows. With well-structured declarative pipelines, refined CI/CD integrations, and clear approval flows, teams can deliver infrastructure changes safely and quickly.

The benefits go beyond the technical team: the business gains predictable operations, fewer incidents, and greater speed to launch new products and services. Knowing common errors and applying best practices ensures resilient pipelines and avoids rework, strengthening the DevOps culture.

CHAPTER 22. DIAGNOSTICS AND DEBUGGING

Diagnostics and debugging are fundamental steps for maintaining stable operations, reducing incident response time, and ensuring the continuity of automated pipelines and infrastructure with Terraform. It's not enough to simply apply commands and hope for success: mature teams know how to interpret logs, analyze unexpected behaviors, and use external tools to identify failure points precisely. This chapter explores how to enable and use debug logs, conduct failure analysis, integrate external tools, resolve common errors, and apply best practices that strengthen resilience and operational efficiency. We close with a strategic summary highlighting the importance of these practices in the organizational context.

Debug Logs

Terraform offers native features to increase log verbosity, allowing investigation of execution problems, from authentication failures to unexpected behaviors in provisioned resources.

Enabling debug logs

Terraform uses the TF_LOG environment variable to control log detail level:

- TRACE: most detailed level, including all events.

- DEBUG: extensive technical details, useful for technical analysis.

- INFO: standard informational messages.

- WARN: only warnings and alerts.

- ERROR: only critical errors.

Example of execution with detailed logs:

bash

```
TF_LOG=DEBUG terraform apply
```

It's also recommended to redirect logs to a file for easier later analysis:

bash

```
TF_LOG=DEBUG terraform apply > debug.log 2>&1
```

TF_LOG_PATH

If you want to keep the terminal clean, you can use:

bash

```
export TF_LOG=DEBUG
export TF_LOG_PATH=terraform-debug.log
terraform apply
```

This setup organizes logs into a file without cluttering the terminal output.

Failure Analysis

When something goes wrong in Terraform, efficient failure analysis involves three steps:

- Identify the failure point
  Read the log from bottom to top; the final error usually carries the most relevant clue.

- Differentiate between Terraform and provider failures
  A Terraform error typically involves syntax, dependencies, or state; a provider error indicates problems with the external API (AWS, Azure, GCP).

- Reproduce in a controlled environment
  Create a minimal code block with only the problematic resource and run it in isolation.

Examples of common failures for analysis:

- Error acquiring the state lock: multiple concurrent executions.

- Error parsing .tf files: syntax error in the code.

- Provider authentication failed: invalid credentials or token expiration.

- Resource already exists: attempt to recreate an already existing resource.

External Tools

External tools help diagnose problems beyond Terraform, including dependencies, network, and APIs.

Ping, traceroute, curl

Useful for testing connectivity with external endpoints configured in Terraform.

bash

curl https://api.cloudprovider.com/status

ping endpoint

API CLIs (AWS CLI, az CLI, gcloud)

Test direct interactions with the provider:

bash
aws ec2 describe-instances

az vm list

gcloud compute instances list

Terraform validate, plan, and graph

- o   terraform validate: **checks if configuration is correct.**

- o   terraform plan: **simulates changes.**

terraform graph: **generates a visual graph of dependencies.**

bash
terraform graph | dot -Tpng > graph.png

checkov, tfsec

Security tools that help identify configuration errors that may not block deployment but pose risks.

Common Error Resolution

Error: Error locking state
Cause: concurrent execution or state not released.

Solution: use terraform force-unlock with the lock ID to manually release the state.

Error: Dependency cycle detected
Cause: resources referencing each other.
Solution: restructure the code, use depends_on explicitly if necessary.

Error: Provider not installed
Cause: missing plugins in the directory.
Solution: run terraform init to download and initialize providers.

Error: Timeout during apply
Cause: timeout reached when creating a resource.
Solution: increase timeouts in the resource blocks (timeouts), investigate provider limitations.

Error: Authentication failed
Cause: expired keys, incorrect permissions.
Solution: update credentials, test the connection with the native CLI, check roles and policies.

Best Practices

- Enable logs only when necessary to avoid overload.

- Store critical logs in centralized repositories (S3, Cloud Storage, Blob Storage) for auditing.

- Use terraform validate on every pull request.

- Simulate changes with terraform plan before applying.

- Automate security checks with checkov and tfsec in CI/CD.

- Reduce problematic resources to minimal blocks during

debugging.

- Document error patterns and solutions in an internal repository.

- Periodically review backend and locking configuration.

- Train the team to interpret logs and structure collaborative debugging.

- Use terraform console to inspect values in the state.

Strategic Summary

Diagnostics and debugging with Terraform are crucial differentiators for keeping operations stable, reducing incident response time, and anticipating problems before they hit critical environments. Enabling detailed logs, knowing how to conduct an organized analysis, using external tools, and adopting robust validation and linting practices make the environment more resilient and ready to scale.

More than just solving failures, the ability to understand and anticipate problems transforms IT teams into strategic business partners. This means less time lost on repetitive errors, more predictability in deliveries, and greater confidence from stakeholders.

CHAPTER 23. SCALABILITY AND PERFORMANCE

Scalability and performance are indispensable aspects in modern Terraform operations, especially as environments grow to dozens or hundreds of resources distributed across multiple regions, providers, and environments. Poorly optimized Terraform code can lead to slowness, crashes, and even wasted cloud resources. Working efficiently means building optimized scripts, intelligently modularizing code, managing parallel executions, and quickly resolving bottlenecks as infrastructure scales.

Script Tuning

Tuning Terraform scripts begins with a careful code review to ensure it's clean, concise, and avoids unnecessary operations.

Simplifying expressions

Avoid complex calculations and excessive logic in .tf files; prefer preprocessing data outside of Terraform when possible.

hcl

```
variable "region" {
  default = "us-east-1"
}
```

Instead of embedding long expressions:

hcl

```
locals {
  full_region = "${var.region}-az1"
}
```

Prefer using simple and direct locals.

Selective outputs

Avoid excessive outputs, which can impact performance and increase state file size.

hcl

```
output "vpc_id" {
  value = aws_vpc.main.id
}
```

Only expose data truly needed for use in pipelines or external scripts.

Reducing resources during test cycles

During testing and development, limit the number of resources created using conditional variables or workspaces to speed up the plan → apply cycle.

Efficient Modularization

Good modularization is key to maintaining performance and organization as code grows.

Domain-based separation

Split modules by logical domain: network, security, compute, storage, observability.

pgsql

```
modules/
```

├── network/

├── compute/

├── storage/

├── security/

Reuse with parameters

Configure modules to receive generic variables to enable reuse:

hcl

```
module "network" {
  source   = "./modules/network"
  cidr_block = "10.0.0.0/16"
}
```

Environment separation

Separate environments (dev, stage, prod) by directory or workspace, avoiding overload and accidental changes across environments.

Avoid excessive coupling

Use outputs and inputs clearly between modules without creating unnecessary interdependencies.

Parallel Management

Terraform performs operations in parallel to accelerate execution, but this must be managed carefully.

Parallelism configuration

The -parallelism parameter controls the number of simultaneous operations.

bash

```
terraform apply -parallelism=10
```

Increasing this value helps in large environments, but may overload provider APIs.

Using depends_on

When order must be guaranteed, use depends_on explicitly to avoid failures in parallel executions.

hcl

```
resource "aws_instance" "web" {
  depends_on = [aws_security_group.web_sg]
}
```

Optimized backend

Ensure that the backend (S3, GCS, Azure Blob) supports locking and efficient parallel operations.

Common Error Resolution

Error: Rate limit exceeded
Cause: Excessive parallel execution exceeding provider API limits.
Solution: Reduce -parallelism value and, if possible, request quota increase from provider.

Error: Resource already exists
Cause: Concurrent execution without order control.
Solution: Properly configure depends_on and ensure unique names.

Error: State file too large

Cause: Accumulation of resources and outputs in state.
Solution: Reduce outputs, split state by environment or module, use workspaces.

Error: Long plan/apply times
Cause: Non-modularized code, excessive dependencies.
Solution: Restructure the project into modules and execute in parts when possible.

Error: Lock timeout
Cause: Simultaneous executions on the same state.
Solution: Configure a remote backend with robust locking and serialize critical executions.

Best Practices

- Modularize by domain and environment, not just by provider.

- Use -parallelism in a balanced way: increase for performance gains, but monitor API limits.

- Configure outputs only when necessary to reduce state pollution.

- Use terraform graph to visualize dependencies and identify bottlenecks.

- Adopt workspaces to isolate environments and reduce state size.

- Clearly document module structure and dependencies.

- Monitor CI/CD pipeline performance and adjust parallelism accordingly.

- Use linting tools (like tflint) to keep code clean and

efficient.

- Perform periodic reviews to refactor modules that have grown too large.

- Audit backend configuration to ensure it supports high load.

Strategic Summary

The scalability and performance of a Terraform project depend not just on the cloud or the resources, but on code quality, modular architecture, and intelligent use of parallel capabilities. Adjusting scripts, modularizing efficiently, and managing parallel executions ensures infrastructure can grow sustainably without compromising delivery speed or operational stability.

A team that masters these practices can accelerate provisioning, reduce operational costs, and increase predictability of changes, transforming operations into a strategic engine for the business. Knowing and resolving common errors helps prevent critical outages and promotes continuous improvement.

CHAPTER 24. CLOUD COST OPTIMIZATION

Optimizing cloud costs with Terraform is an essential practice to avoid waste, control budgets, and ensure infrastructure investments align with business objectives. As environments scale in size and complexity, the risk of hidden costs or underutilized resources increases exponentially. A well-planned Terraform project can not only provision resources efficiently but also include mechanisms for control, tracking, and waste elimination. This chapter explores the pillars of cost analysis, the use of tags and labels, practical recommendations to reduce expenses, resolution of common errors, and best practices to maintain a lean and sustainable operation. The closing section provides a strategic summary connecting these actions to tangible impacts on organizational performance.

Cost Analysis

Cost analysis begins with full visibility over provisioned resources. Native cloud provider tools should be integrated into the management pipeline.

AWS Cost Explorer

Allows analysis of usage and costs by service, tag, region, and period.

bash

```
aws ce get-cost-and-usage --time-period
Start=2023-01-01,End=2023-01-31 --granularity MONTHLY --
metrics BlendedCost
```

Google Cloud Billing Reports

Provides detailed reports with filters by project and label.

bash

```
gcloud beta billing accounts list
```

Azure Cost Management + Billing

Offers consumption dashboards by subscription and resource group.

In Terraform, using terraform show and terraform state list helps inventory deployed resources and compare them against financial reports. Additionally, many providers offer APIs that can be consumed by Terraform scripts or external tools to generate automated reports.

Use of Tags and Labels

Tags and labels are fundamental for tracking, categorizing, and controlling costs. They allow grouping of resources by project, environment, cost center, team, or application.

AWS

hcl

```
resource "aws_instance" "web" {
  tags = {
    Environment = "prod"
    Owner     = "devops-team"
    CostCenter = "finance"
  }
}
```

Google Cloud

hcl

```hcl
resource "google_compute_instance" "web" {
  labels = {
    environment = "prod"
    owner    = "devops-team"
    costcenter = "finance"
  }
}
```

Azure

hcl

```hcl
resource "azurerm_virtual_machine" "web" {
  tags = {
    Environment = "prod"
    Owner    = "devops-team"
    CostCenter = "finance"
  }
}
```

These markings should be standardized and mandatory in all Terraform modules, ensuring traceability during invoice analysis.

Practical Recommendations

- Use reserved instances or savings plans for predictable workloads.

- Adopt autoscaling to automatically adjust resources based on demand.

- Choose appropriate machine types; the largest model is not always the most cost-effective.

- Shut down non-production environments after business hours.

- Configure expiration policies (TTL) for temporary environments.

- Optimize storage with classes like S3 Glacier, Google Coldline, or Azure Cool Storage for rarely accessed data.

- Monitor network traffic to avoid excessive costs from cross-region transfers.

- Use reusable modules to reduce code duplication and inconsistencies that cause waste.

Resolution of Common Errors

Error: Missing tags on resources
Cause: Tags not defined in Terraform code.
Solution: Add tags in the tags or labels block and set them as required variables in the module.

Error: Unused resources left running
Cause: Temporary environments not removed.
Solution: Configure terraform destroy routines in pipelines or use TTL in modules.

Error: Overprovisioned instances
Cause: Use of larger machines than necessary.
Solution: Monitor metrics and downgrade instances.

Error: Storage costs unexpectedly high
Cause: Missing lifecycle policies on buckets or disks.
Solution: Apply lifecycle rules to move or delete old objects.

Error: Traffic between regions too expensive
Cause: Poorly planned architecture with cross-region communication.
Solution: Reorganize resources to reduce inter-region or zone traffic.

Best Practices

- Establish a standardized naming convention for tags and labels organization-wide.

- Create Terraform policies that reject code without required tags.

- Use tools like Infracost to predict costs before applying changes.

- Automate cost report generation with scripts or APIs.

- Adopt serverless architecture where possible to reduce idle server expenses.

- Enable alerts in the provider console for excessive consumption.

- Conduct periodic cost reviews with engineering and finance teams.

- Establish clear ownership for each environment or project.

- Document optimization decisions for traceability.

- Educate teams on the financial impact of each resource.

Strategic Summary

Cloud cost optimization is not just about financial savings but also about operational responsibility and strategic alignment between technology and business. Incorporating cost analysis practices, tag standardization, automated reporting, and continuous review reduces waste, increases budget predictability, and strengthens collaboration between technical and financial teams.

When teams apply the right recommendations and maintain a constant discipline of review and adjustment, they can extract maximum value from the cloud without negative surprises. Knowing and resolving common errors avoids dangerous deviations, while best practices create a sustainable and efficient environment.

CHAPTER 25. CASE STUDIES

Case studies are fundamental for transforming theory into practice, showing how complex architectures can be implemented, what challenges arise along the way, and what lessons can be drawn for future projects. When applying Terraform to large-scale projects, especially in multi-cloud scenarios, practical experience becomes even more relevant. This module presents two emblematic cases: multi-cloud deployment with Terraform and the complete DataExtreme project. It also highlights lessons learned, the most common errors encountered in these contexts, best practices extracted from these experiences, and a strategic summary that connects these practices to organizational impact.

Multi-Cloud Deployment

Multi-cloud deployment with Terraform combines resources from providers like AWS, Google Cloud, and Azure into a single integrated architecture. This approach meets demands for global high availability, vendor lock-in risk mitigation, and regulatory compliance across regions.

Case Objectives

- Provision VPCs in AWS, GCP, and Azure.

- Configure global load balancers.

- Distribute workloads across different clouds.

- Centralize monitoring.

Architecture

- AWS → EC2 for processing and S3 for storage.

- Google Cloud → GKE for container orchestration.

- Azure → Azure SQL for managed database.

Terraform Code

```hcl
provider "aws" {
  region = "us-east-1"
}


provider "google" {
  region = "us-central1"
}


provider "azurerm" {
  features {}
}


# AWS EC2
resource "aws_instance" "web" {
  ami          = "ami-0c55b159cbfafe1f0"
  instance_type = "t3.micro"
```

```
}


# Google GKE
resource "google_container_cluster" "primary" {
  name         = "gke-cluster"
  location     = "us-central1"
  initial_node_count = 3
}


# Azure SQL
resource "azurerm_mssql_server" "main" {
  name                = "sqlserver-multicloud"
  resource_group_name      = "rg"
  location            = "East US"
  version             = "12.0"
  administrator_login      = "adminuser"
  administrator_login_password = var.sql_password
}
```

Results

- Resources provisioned consistently across clouds.

- Unified operation with remote backend.

- Integrated monitoring via Prometheus and Grafana.

DataExtreme Project Example

The DataExtreme project was designed to orchestrate massive cloud data pipelines, integrating collection, processing, analysis, and visualization.

Case Objectives

- Provision automatic ETL pipelines.

- Integrate Airflow, Spark, and BigQuery.

- Ensure scalability and high availability.

- Reduce costs with optimized architecture.

Provisioned Components

- GCP → BigQuery and Cloud Storage.

- AWS → EMR with Spark.

- Azure → Airflow with Azure Kubernetes Service (AKS).

Execution Flow

- Airflow on AKS schedules pipelines.

- Spark on EMR processes data.

- BigQuery stores results.

- Grafana connects to BigQuery for real-time visualization.

Terraform Code

hcl

```hcl
# Google BigQuery
resource "google_bigquery_dataset" "dataset" {
  dataset_id = "dataextreme"
  location   = "US"
}


# AWS EMR
resource "aws_emr_cluster" "emr_cluster" {
  name          = "emr-dataextreme"
  release_label = "emr-6.3.0"
  applications  = ["Spark"]
}


# Azure AKS
resource "azurerm_kubernetes_cluster" "aks" {
  name                = "aks-airflow"
  location            = "East US"
  resource_group_name = "rg"
  dns_prefix          = "airflow"
}
```

Results

- 35% reduction in computational costs.

- Processing of 10 TB/day with 99.9% availability.

- End-to-end traceable pipelines.

Lessons Learned

- **Importance of remote backend:** Without a remote backend, multi-cloud management is impractical.

- **Need for modularization:** Reusable modules reduce deployment time and errors.

- **Disciplined use of tags and labels:** Critical for cost analysis and troubleshooting.

- **Automated testing and linting:** Essential for maintaining code quality in multi-team environments.

- **Proactive monitoring:** Anticipating problems reduces impacts and avoids critical incidents.

Resolution of Common Errors

Error: Provider authentication failure
Cause: Credentials not configured or token expiration.
Solution: Configure environment variables, profiles, or use secret vaults.

Error: State locking conflicts
Cause: Simultaneous executions without proper locking.
Solution: Enable locking in the remote backend.

Error: Resource name conflicts
Cause: Globally non-unique resource names.
Solution: Use dynamic variables and suffixes in the code.

Error: Cross-provider dependency issues
Cause: Resources from one provider depending on another without explicit wait.
Solution: Properly configure depends_on.

Error: Cost overruns due to drift
Cause: Manual changes in the environment outside of Terraform.
Solution: Run terraform refresh and avoid changes outside the code.

Best Practices

- Split environments (dev, stage, prod) with workspaces or directories.

- Standardize names for modules, variables, and outputs.

- Automate validation with terraform validate and linting with tflint.

- Use CI/CD pipelines to orchestrate multi-cloud.

- Adopt a remote backend with locking enabled.

- Set up cost and usage alerts to avoid surprises.

- Integrate log and metric monitoring.

- Conduct periodic code and architecture reviews.

- Document the provisioning flow and dependencies.

- Promote internal training on multi-cloud practices.

Strategic Summary

Case studies such as the multi-cloud deployment and the DataExtreme project show that Terraform goes far beyond simple provisioning: it transforms how teams operate in global, complex, and interdependent environments. The ability to create, modularize, and manage heterogeneous environments consistently provides not only technical efficiency but also a strategic competitive advantage.

Lessons learned, resolved errors, and applied best practices consolidate a mature operation capable of growing without compromising stability or predictability. Professionals who master these scenarios not only deliver complex projects but also position their organizations at the forefront of digital innovation, connecting technology, business, and outcomes in a continuous cycle of evolution and improvement.

FINAL CONCLUSION

Throughout this learning journey on Terraform, we explored a path that spanned from basic to advanced topics, preparing any professional to face the challenges of modern infrastructure with confidence, organization, and precision. Consolidating these concepts, chapter by chapter, not only allows knowledge retention but also enables understanding of how each piece fits into a larger ecosystem of automation and efficiency.

We began with a fundamental introduction to Terraform, understanding what it represents within the concept of Infrastructure as Code (IaC). This start was essential to recognize the benefits and use cases that justify adopting this powerful tool, positioning it within the context of corporate and operational demands. We also explored the ecosystem surrounding Terraform, recognizing that it does not operate in isolation but as part of a mechanism that connects operations, development, and business teams.

We then moved on to the installation process, focusing on proper downloading, PATH configuration, and executing the first command. This step was crucial to enable any beginner to get the tool running in a local environment, gaining familiarity with the first commands and consolidating the confidence needed to advance.

With the foundation established, we delved into the fundamental concepts: providers, resources, variables, and outputs. This theoretical layer provided the understanding of how the basic components relate and form the backbone of any infrastructure created with Terraform. We also discussed modules and state, reinforcing the importance of the basic execution cycle and state preservation to ensure consistency and predictability in environments.

The first Terraform script marked a practical turning point: we learned how to structure .tf files, use essential commands such as init, plan, apply, and destroy, validate scripts, and fix common errors. This practical moment consolidated previous concepts and opened the door to more elaborate experiments.

Variables and outputs came into play to bring flexibility and dynamism. We studied the different types of variables, the reuse of outputs, and the importance of external variables, always with attention to organization and code clarity. From there, we introduced modules, addressing their creation, reuse across projects, and practical examples, reinforcing the importance of modularization for scalable and easy-to-maintain projects.

State management revealed the critical value of state in collaborative projects, highlighting the difference between local state and remote state, the role of backends, the use of locking, and the necessary attention to state security, as it contains sensitive information.

We advanced to cloud provider integration, starting with AWS, where we explored provider configuration, EC2, S3, RDS deployment, and secure authentication practices. We then addressed Azure integration, configuring providers, deploying VMs, Blob Storage, SQL, and discussing secure key management. Google Cloud integration consolidated the learning, showing the configuration of Compute Engine, Cloud Storage, and BigQuery, as well as authentication via service account.

In network provisioning, we learned how to configure VPCs, subnets, firewall rules, cross-cloud environments, and load balancing—essential elements to ensure high availability and security. Storage provisioning brought buckets, volumes, and snapshots, as well as access policies and multi-cloud scenarios, demonstrating how storage must be carefully planned for performance and cost-effectiveness.

The database chapter covered PostgreSQL and MySQL deployment, backup configuration, user and permission creation, expanding the ability to manage data securely and reliably. Kubernetes cluster deployment introduced cluster provisioning, automatic configuration, integration with Helm, and showed how to orchestrate large-scale applications.

With Airflow pipelines, we understood how to orchestrate complex workflows, configure DAGs, and integrate monitoring. The introduction of MLflow for MLOps demonstrated how to manage experiments, pipelines, and machine learning models, integrating data science into the automation cycle.

Automation with CI/CD was deeply covered with GitHub Actions and GitLab CI, discussing Terraform pipeline construction, test automation, and continuous deployment strategies. In the security and compliance field, we addressed policies, roles, linting, sensitive data protection, and how to keep operations secure and aligned with regulatory best practices.

Monitoring with Prometheus and Grafana highlighted the importance of exporters, dashboards, and automatic alerts to maintain the operational health of environments, while Ansible integration showed how Terraform and Ansible complement each other, enabling provisioning and configuration in a continuous flow. Jenkins integration detailed declarative pipelines, CI/CD integration, and real examples, preparing teams to deliver rapid and controlled changes.

In diagnosis and debugging, we learned to enable debug logs, analyze failures, use external tools, and resolve errors in a structured way. Scalability and performance addressed script tuning, efficient modularization, parallel management, and strategies for dealing with high-complexity environments.

Cloud cost optimization was a crucial chapter for aligning operations with financial results, teaching cost analysis, use of tags and labels, practical recommendations, and tools to control expenses. We concluded with case studies, highlighting the multi-cloud deployment and the DataExtreme project, extracting valuable lessons on remote backend, modularization, tagging, test automation, and proactive monitoring.

Future Directions

The advancement of automation with Terraform is far from a final point. Future directions point to even more sophisticated integrations with artificial intelligence, self-healing pipelines, serverless and edge computing architectures, and the increasing use of tools that offer policy as code to reinforce security and compliance. Teams must prepare to deal with increasingly distributed, mutable, and hybrid environments, strengthening practices of versioning, automated testing, and continuous collaboration. Continuing to evolve means not just mastering new tools but deepening the DevOps mindset, the culture of continuous improvement, and the integration between technology and business purpose.

Final Recommendations

Working with Terraform is much more than writing code. It requires discipline, attention to detail, awareness of dependencies, and a commitment to quality. Every successful project is born from the alignment between people, processes, and tools. It is recommended to document all steps, constantly review the architecture, and maintain a proactive stance in the face of environmental changes. Learning never ends, and every new project is an opportunity to refine patterns, test ideas, and strengthen the technical ecosystem.

To the reader who has followed this journey: thank you very much for your dedication, patience, and curiosity. Each page was written with the goal of offering clarity, usefulness, and inspiration to transform daily work into something more efficient, secure, and strategic. I hope this content has added real value to your practice, sparked new ideas, and strengthened your confidence in the art of building infrastructure as code.

Sincerely,
Diego Rodrigues & Team!

www.ingramcontent.com/pod-product-compliance
Lightning Source LLC
LaVergne TN
LVHW051227050326
832903LV00028B/2281

*9 7 9 8 2 8 2 9 0 7 7 5 9 *